PRAISE FOR THE SIX-FIGURE SPEAKER

W9-BXZ-291

"Based on Cathleen's vast experience as a bureau owner and consultant, combined with interviews with some of the world's top speakers, this book shows you how to create your own blueprint for extreme success. The Six-Figure Speaker is solid gold!"

W Mitchell, CSP, CPAE

"I can't believe how comprehensive The Six-Figure Speaker is. Speakers literally learn everything they need to become successful in a competitive industry where most people don't make it. I especially like how Cathleen included personal stories and advice from dozens of six-figure speakers. If you want to go from struggling to successful speaker, you need this book."

Larina Kase, PsyD, MBA, Co-Author of The Confident Speaker
and Founder of Performance & Success Coaching

"This is a great book that I highly recommend for any speaker at any stage of their career. Cathleen Fillmore has done a brilliant job at creating an incredible resource!"

James Malinchak, Co-Author, Chicken Soup for the College Soul
and Chicken Soup for the Athlete's Soul,
Founder of www.CollegeSpeakingSuccess.com

"The Six-Figure Speaker is a brilliant book that the speaking industry really needs and all speakers must read. This book is like holding the magic key to unlock the doors of knowledge about the speaking industry. You'll find out everything that you need to know to move into the speaking profession fast. Having Cathleen coach you on finding the money in the marketplace is a bonus! Speaking personally, as someone who worked her way up from giving free talks in health food stores to now providing keynotes at conferences around the world, I know firsthand your burning desire as a speaker to command money sooner. The Six-Figure Speaker tells you how."

Terri Levine, author of many books including, The Successful Coach:
Insider Tips to Becoming a Top Coach and Magnetizing

"Cathleen, you're one of the great thinkers in this industry — thanks for sharing!"

Donald Cooper, CSP, Hall of Fame

PRAISE FOR THE SIX-FIGURE SPEAKER

"Cathleen has a way of inspiring greatness in a speaker which helps maximize demand and income. Her words take you to a new level of thought and action. Follow her advice and you will power up your spirit and level of effectiveness. Your audience will simply love you and want more and more."

Joycebelle, GoodStoryADay.com Inc., Author, Speaker, Consultant to mega-bestselling authors Robert Allen and Mark Victor Hansen

"Cathleen's honesty about this industry will arm you with the inside knowledge you need to jump through many hoops faster than you could alone. Using this book as your tool kit brings Cathleen into your life as your cheerleader, coach and oracle as you move into the truth of who you are and how you can share your divine gifts with the world"

Jane Clapp, President, Urbanfitt

"Cathleen, this book is a brilliant resource for all speakers. You show speakers how to burst right through their financial ceilings. This is a must have for established professional speakers and also for those just starting out."

Jill Lublin
International Speaker, Best Selling Author of Guerrilla Publicity

"Cathleen, the depth and range of your expertise is amazing. Keep doing what you're doing – you're changing people's lives."

Susan Sweeney, CSP, Hall of Fame

"Brilliant! The Six-Figure Speaker is a MUST read for all serious minded professional speakers who want to reap great profits from the business of professional speaking. It's essential reading for those who dare to be the 'Best of the Best'. Cathleen has broken the code."

Brigadier General (CA) (Retired) Ezell Ware, Jr.
Author and Professional Speaker

"The Six-Figure Speaker has the inside track on finding the money in the conference market. As bureau owner and consultant, Cathleen knows this industry inside-out. A wealth of information – I highly recommend it.

Bill Cates, CSP, Author of Get More Referrals Now

The
SIX
FIGURE
Speaker

*Formula for a Six-Figure Income
as a Professional Speaker*

Cathleen Fillmore

Robert D. Reed Publishers
P.O. Box 1992
Bandon, OR 97411
Phone: 541-347-9882; Fax: -9883
E-mail: 4bobreed@msn.com
Website: www.rdrpublishers.com

Editor: Peggy Amirault
Cover Designer: Mait Ainsaar, BICN Marketing & Design
Photographer: Author's photo by Yuri Dojc
Typesetter: Mait Ainsaar, BICN Marketing & Design

ISBN: 978-1-931741-92-7

Library of Congress Number: 2007934873

Manufactured and Printed in the United States of America

Important Disclaimer: The Six-Figure Speaker is designed to provide accurate and authoritative information in regard to professional speaking. This book is sold with the understanding that the author, contributors and publisher are not responsible for the results of any action taken on the basis of information in this work, nor for any errors or omissions. The publisher and the author and contributors expressly disclaim all and any liability to any person whether a purchaser of this publication or not, in respect of anything and of the consequences of anything done or omitted to be done by any such person in reliance, whether whole or partial, upon the whole or any part of the contents of this publication.

ACKNOWLEDGEMENTS

It certainly takes a village to write a book and my village has been populated with superb team players. First of all, a huge thank you to the indomitable Mait Ainsaar who designed the cover and formatted the book. Great job, Mait, I'm eternally grateful.

Thanks to Orvel Ray Wilson, CSP, who took time away from a very busy life to write the foreword and give me feedback on the manuscript.

I am deeply indebted to all the speakers who gave freely of their time and shared their strategies with no other purpose except to help others climb the speaking ladder.

Thanks also to Peggy Amirault. She went way beyond the bounds of duty in her proofreading and did excellent work.

I appreciate my publisher Robert Reed not only for his sage advice but also for his speedy response to my query.

Thanks to Garry Schleiffer and Katie Curtin for their patience, wisdom and coaching advice. Thanks always to Adam, Ailyn, Damian and Evan for their ongoing love, encouragement and support.

Finally, I'm deeply grateful to all my clients over the years for making me a partner on their splendid and sometimes breathtaking journeys. I have learned just how many ways there are to succeed when the determination is there. You're the real reason I'm in this business and in a constant state of inspiration.

This book is dedicated to each and every one of you.

Cathleen

TABLE OF CONTENTS

FOREWORD

By Orvel Ray Wilson, CSP
The Guerrilla Marketing Group

You may not know this, but most professional speakers fail. They fail their audiences, they fail their families, and they fail their bankers. Fully a third of the membership in the National Speakers Association turns over annually. That's a thousand people every year who give up speaking and get a job.

It's common knowledge that most small businesses fail, some just get by, while a few are wildly successful. In this respect, professional speaking is no different. Like many of this book's contributors, I have failed miserably as a speaker, and experienced success beyond my wildest dreams. The lessons learned are all here.

But if all you want to do is make a six-figure income, then being a speaker is not the best way to go about it. It's difficult. Being a speaker takes as much time as running a restaurant and as much stamina as running a marathon. It requires more research than a PhD, and cleanses your spirit like a Tibetan trek. It can open up the world to you and it will bare your soul to the world. It can make you rich, while costing you your marriage, your family and your health.

It's complicated. A professional speaker is part teacher, part poet, part journalist, part performer, part comedian, part AV tech and part travel agent. You are a story-teller, a fact-finder, a problem-solver. You must challenge, involve, inform, inspire, educate, entertain and motivate your audience, all at the same time. You must simultaneously appear to be calm and confident, energized and excited, educated and ordinary, exceptional and approachable. You must deliver your message with the passion of a sermon, the conviction of a pastor, and the political correctness of a pulpit. The Six-Figure Speaker earns every dime.

For some, stepping onto the stage is terrifying; for others, it's transformational. Speaking will bring out the best in you, and the worst. It can turn you into an arrogant prima donna by day, and a lonely whimpering child at night. A speaker basks in the spotlight, the focus of attention and adulation for hours at a stretch. We tell jokes and stories, talking about the books we've read, the people we've known, the things we've seen.

At the end they stand and applaud and cheer, then corner you for

i

personal advice and personalized autographs. But then there is no emptiness in the cosmos like looking out into that huge ballroom as you pack your props and product, house lights up, chairs askew, tables littered with dirty coffee cups and abandoned handouts. A few minutes ago you a star. Now you're just another anonymous fare going to the airport. The Six-Figure Speaker must be both soft-hearted and mentally tough.

The platform is a great leveler, where real-world experience trumps an ivory tower sheepskin. Some have earned the right to speak by succeeding in business or politics or sports. Some are authors, and therefore, authorities. Some have overcome terrible adversity in their lives and so have a compelling personal story to tell. The high school dropout is often more riveting than the speaker with multiple masters' degrees. The Six-Figure Speaker doesn't need to be an MVP in the NFL, lose multiple limbs while climbing Everest, or sell a million books. It can't hurt, but there's more to it. Your six-figure value comes from finding the extraordinary in ordinary things, and showing us ordinary folks how to overcome everyday adversity with day-to-day heroism.

Some speakers do it for the adventure, some for the applause. Some do it for the message and some for the money. Some speakers love to travel; others are loath to leave home. Some speak to fill the minds and hearts of their audiences. Others speak to fill some empty space inside themselves. Some speakers put on a show with lights, music, and animated PowerPoint. Others captivate the whole hall with just the quiet sound of their voices. Some speakers abuse the stage by bragging about great things they've done. The Six-Figure Speaker inspires confidence in the rest of us to do great things ourselves.

Certainly there are much simpler ways to get rich. In fact, if you're only in it for the money then get out while you're ahead. Don't get me wrong. I've made millions as a speaker. But this is one profession where your net worth increases proportional to your personal growth. To become a Six-Figure Speaker you must constantly invest in yourself.

Most speakers don't bother. Instead they tell the same shopworn stories again and again. They work in anecdotes about flying first class, staying in five-star hotels, and then have the hubris to complain about the room service. That makes them sound lazy and vain. If you're a Six-Figure Speaker, you stay up late reading the annual reports and you study the product and the process until you sound like you're from home office. Six-Figure Speakers offer answers, solutions and hope.

In more than a quarter-century of speaking professionally, I've made every mistake imaginable, learned most of these lessons the hard way, and still managed to earn a six-figure income along the way. If you're ready to commit yourself to being truly exceptional, then this book is for you. It will cut years off your learning curve, and add years to your earning curve. It will put you on the road to becoming a Six-Figure Speaker.

Orvel Ray Wilson, CSP, www.theguerrillagroup.com

INTRODUCTION

Why You Should Read This Book

Congratulations!

You've just invested in a crash course on how to make big money as a professional speaker.

Let's be honest. Most speakers work far too hard for far too little for much too long. And those who depend solely on speaking for their income are vulnerable to the ups and downs of the marketplace.

You'll hear about speakers who have succeeded although you wouldn't have bet a nickel on them when they started out. Multi-millionaire speakers and entrepreneurs Chris Widener and Jack Zufelt began with nothing. Except their bare hands and raw talent. That turned out to be enough. The truth is people with tremendous odds against them earn fantastic incomes while others with everything in their favor still struggle. Curious, isn't it?

You'll look below the surface to discover why. In this book, North America's top professional speakers openly share the secrets of their success and how they propelled themselves to the top. They also tell you about the mistakes they made and what they did to overcome the occasional absolute disaster.

You'll benefit from their learning curves and shorten your own as you take a more profitable, secure and diversified route. You'll follow in the footsteps of the few who've managed to make this challenging yet exciting profession work well for them. Really well!

There are no holds barred in this book.

Reading The Six-Figure Speaker will put money in your pocket if you're a coach/trainer wanting to add another income stream or if you are really serious about busting through the financial ceiling in your speaking career.

Serious is the operative word. Unless you're serious, you won't succeed. If you're not ready to move ahead, you might as well put this book down. This field takes dedication and perseverance above all else.

I've dedicated the past ten years to the speaking profession and openly share with you all I've learned from starting and operating a busy bureau, building a thriving consulting practice and interviewing the top-income speakers. No matter where you are in your speaking career, the information contained within these covers will open your eyes to new possibilities and take your career to an exciting new level.

Are you ready for it?

It takes talent, time, dedication, perseverance and enthusiasm to be a top level professional speaker with a solid six-figure-and-beyond income. It won't happen by accident. You'll look at every aspect of your business as you map out your winning strategy.

Taking things to the next level requires that you stretch yourself and go beyond your current comfort zone. You'll dream much larger dreams, model yourself after the big players and move right into the future you've always wanted.

You'll discover your own winning formula for a six-figure income that is breathtaking in its simplicity and brilliant in its scope. It will keep you absolutely on track to achieve those massive dreams.

On time, on target.

It all starts with managing those two precious commodities - your attitude and your time. So let's not waste another minute.

Thank you for making The Six-Figure Speaker part of your winning strategy. Get a notebook and grab your favorite pen – you'll get the most out of this book if you begin to create or recreate a brand new plan for moving forward as you read each chapter.

Unplug the phone and set aside time right now to settle in and read. Strap yourself in – your speaking career is about to go to new heights. You might need altitude pills.

I assure you, you'll make more money by reading this book and revamping your marketing strategy than you will by continuing to keep your nose to the grindstone. So shut down the office for a couple of days as you re-evaluate and create a new business model.

Please don't just read this book and put it down. Read it slowly and put an action plan into place as you go. I know that only a small percentage of you will actually implement these ideas. Good for you - you'll be the next Six and Seven Figure Speakers!

Let me know of your successes. I'd love to include your story in my next book.

Best Wishes for a Dazzling Career!

Cathleen Fillmore

CHAPTER 1

The Top of the Mountain

"I'm going to the top of the mountain. You are either going to see me waving from the top or dead on the side. But you know what? I'm not coming down."

Eric Worre, author, speaker

This quote really struck me. So hard, in fact, it took my breath away. I wanted to stand up and cheer for Eric Worre, whether or not he ever climbed a real mountain. Because we've all climbed mountains of some sort. Not always with that absolute deadly determination though.

Every time I read that quote, I get a buzz from it. It is reminiscent of the way I felt when I sold my house, packed up my car and moved to Nova Scotia 10 years ago for a career change. I had no clue where I was going to live or what exactly I was going to do.

I'm serious. No clue. I had some ideas floating around my head but that was it.

As the amazing speaker Suzie Humphreys so famously says "Well, how hard could it BE?" I was about to find out.

All I knew was that I was running for my life. I was running to recapture my life.

I remember saying to myself as I left everything behind and pulled onto the highway, holding on hard to the steering wheel as though it were a lifeline, "I'm going to reinvent myself. And if it doesn't work out, I can always walk into the ocean."

That may sound like a death wish, but it's actually a very life-affirming statement. It's saying, "I'm going to do this. Or else." It's saying, "Failure is NOT an option." It's an expression of total absolute determination.

Failure is not doing something and not succeeding. I define failure as saying to yourself (and I've done it many times) "Oh, I'll never make it to the top. Might as well quit now and turn around." That is failure in the form of abdication. Whenever we make that false statement to

1

ourselves, we're walking away from the prize. Occasionally, that's a smart decision. Most of the time, that's failure, pure and simple.

Failure is focusing on the difficulties and underestimating our abilities to overcome them. W Mitchell could be forgiven for doing that.

Most of us have heard of Mitchell who suffered burns to 65% of his body in a motorcycle accident. Then, he was involved in a plane crash and paralyzed from the waist down. His attitude has been his healing.

He says, "Before my accident, there were 10,000 things I could do. Now there are 9,000. Why should I concentrate on the 1,000 things I can't do instead of focusing on the 9,000 I can do?"

Today Mitchell travels the world spreading his message of hope. He claims, "It's not what happens to you in life, it's what you do about it."

Although he's in a wheelchair and his feet don't hit the ground, W Mitchell is hitting the ground in a big way. He's following in the footsteps of some illustrious predecessors, going way back to Ancient Rome where orators such as Cicero rose to the top of the pack.

Mitchell's also following the lead of King Henry V of England whose troops were hopelessly outnumbered when they were about to face French soldiers in the Battle of Agincourt in fifteenth-century Normandy.

The night before the battle, Henry convinced his exhausted soldiers that they would go down in history and everyone would envy the "band of brothers" who valiantly fought this battle.

Ten thousand French soldiers were killed that next day and only 28 of Henry's men.

That demonstrates the power of the spoken word.

Paid professional speakers began to emerge in America at the turn of the nineteenth century. Speakers such as Daniel Webster, Ralph Waldo Emerson, Oliver Wendell Holmes and Henry Ward Beecher were paid in the range of $10 or $20, although Beecher commanded an exorbitant $250 for his appearances.

These pioneers paved the way for new generations of professional speakers to follow. And follow they did, upping the ante with each generation. Baptist minister Russell Conwell earned enough giving his talk "Acres of Diamonds" several hundred times a year to found and fund Temple University.

Other noteworthy speakers who came later were the legendary W. Clement Stone, who partnered with Napoleon Hill to publish 'Success Through a Positive Mental Attitude', Dale Carnegie and Norman Vincent Peale. And we can't forget Cavett Robert, the founder of the National Speakers Association which set off Speakers Associations around the world.

Tony Robbins walked in the footsteps of these giants and built an empire around his book, his speeches and his video training sessions.

Many have tried and failed to adopt Robbins's business model.

2

That particular model of building an empire on motivation alone has been exhausted. It takes a lot of effort to continuously try to animate people. Speakers can't go home with the audience to cheer them on when they get discouraged.

These days there's a more effective way to become a top-paid speaker. Working with motivated clients, getting them to see possibilities they'd missed and mistakes they're currently making and giving them some tools to take a new direction is a route that will never go out of fashion. It's called providing good solid value to your clients and it will last long after your speech.

That's the road you want to take. You already know you haven't chosen this career path because it's an easy route. In fact, let's admit it. Part of the appeal is the challenge.

As Robert Allen says, there are two doors ahead of you. One is named Security and the other is named Freedom. Your choice. Just remember that the door marked Security lies. Professional speakers know that security is an inside job and that freedom is found by following your destiny.

It's your responsibility to remain committed to the process, to remain positive and to be absolutely 100% determined. If you fulfill those three requirements, then truly failure is not an option.

Now what are you planning to do to take your speaking career to the very top? Lace up your hiking boots. Let's go wave from the top of that mountain. I know I intend to. Join me. The view is splendid. Even better when you've got company!

CHAPTER 2

What Drives Your Economic Engine?

"Nothing can add more power to your life than concentrating all of your energies on a limited set of targets."
Nido Qubein, speaker, author, philanthropist

Let me ask you a question – how's business?

Are you a professional speaker or do you run a business?

The answer has to be both.

Some people get carried away with the glamour of being a professional speaker and the joy of addressing large crowds while far fewer focus on building a great speaking business by providing solid value to their clients. Those few are the ones who will succeed financially.

In the end, it's the business that you can bank on.

What is it that drives your economic engine? You may be doing a number of things in your speaking career that are rewarding but where's the money? Is it in the actual speaking? Consulting? Training? Product Sales? Getting clients for your business when you deliver a speech?

I begin my work with clients by finding out where they're making their money at that moment. The answer is often in training, so we create a plan to strengthen that foundation as they make a shift from training to keynote speaking.

While it may not be glamorous, you need to always keep your eye on that bottom line and make income a priority as you build your business. Don't turn down a paid activity for an unpaid speaking gig or take time away from work that pays the bills to send out yet another press release (unless it's part of a very well thought-out strategy).

In other words, put your mouth where the money is. Find the money in the marketplace.

Let's face it, there are those out there gathering a ton of publicity while others are quietly making a pile of money from speaking. You've never heard of them. They probably don't care. Keep your eye on the bottom line! If you don't, you're out of business.

The first step in building your six-figure speaking business is to tell yourself the truth about your strengths and your limitations and build a business model based on that self-knowledge.

We are all brilliant at certain things yet we have areas where we don't do so well. The common wisdom is "Delegate what you don't do well." Since this is a book for uncommon people, I'm going to contradict that by saying "No!" Or at least, "Not yet!"

Don't allow yourself to have huge limitations. For example, if I'm handicapped in the area of accounting and bookkeeping, should I farm all my accounts out to someone else?

Well, it's tempting but that's a great way to create huge headaches for my bookkeeper and myself. I could be robbed blind and never know the difference. I've just completely abdicated my role as financial manager of my own business.

If I have trouble writing, should I farm that out? Not until I learn the basics because otherwise how will I know when someone else does a great job? How will I know if I'm being overcharged by a supplier unless I know what's involved in the job?

We are born with natural talents and inclinations. Great. Now we need to balance our personalities by becoming at least competent in areas where we're weak.

You're running a business. In the beginning, that means you need to be President, Treasurer and Assistant and you need to play all three roles reasonably competently if not brilliantly. So discover what you're really brilliant at; look clearly at what your limitations are and then work to achieve a certain level of competence in all areas as you focus on and enhance your brilliance. You're expanding yourself and adding a little balance to your personality. That has to be a good thing.

So often I have speakers tell me they're no good at marketing and they're anxious to hand marketing over to a third party as though it were a hot potato. They virtually jump in my lap and say, "Market me, market me!" That's a big mistake. I've never seen it work, not once, no matter how compelling their speech is or how polished their platform skills are.

By all means, create a marketing team but you need to market yourself. The only speakers I can create a great marketing plan for are those who are willing to partner with me, who make me a member of their team and who inspire me with their enthusiasm.

If you're not completely enthusiastic about what you do and getting your message out there, then you haven't really discovered your brilliance. Or you haven't found the right way to articulate that to buyers.

Because once you do, you'll be unstoppable. And you'll learn to market yourself even though it may not come naturally. Once you use the right language, marketing will become a breeze.

When you have arrived at that point, you can then delegate it to someone else so you can devote your time to doing what you do best and what only you can do.

When Cork Walgreen, head of Walgreen's drugstore, was asked how the company achieved such great success, he hesitated before replying, "Look, it just wasn't that complicated. Once we understood the concept, we just moved straight ahead."

And the concept? Simply to be the best most convenient drugstores with high profit per customer visit.

The concept is brilliant in its simplicity.

How could you apply this principle to your speaking business?

Are you the best speaker, providing the best value for your clients?

Are you approachable and easy to work with?

What would it mean to you, as a speaker, to be the best in your field and your market? You have heavy competition on the lower end of the scale and very little at the top. Why not go where the field is less crowded? What do you need to do to make yourself absolutely stand out?

And how can you increase, even multiply, your profit per client? By adding products and other add-ons, by building a referral system, by doing a follow-up, by leading a boot camp, by cross-promoting non-competing colleagues, by creating and franchising training videos? There are a lot of different ways limited only by the imagination. So unleash your imagination and start to think about what would work for you.

Take a minute now to think about it. What is your Unique Sales Proposition? What do you stand for that is truly different? What can you do to sweep the marketplace?

When sales trainer Ben Canini wanted to move into the professional speaking arena, he and I worked together on his positioning. The banner we ended up with was "Not Just Another Suit" which I felt expressed Ben's personality perfectly. That positioning statement led to a great photograph which is so outstanding that Conference Online (www.conferenceonline.com.au) chose to feature it on the newsletter they sent out to their massive database. Go to www.inspirationalspeaker.ca to check out it out.

Business coach Paul Lemberg spent a lot of time crafting his unique selling proposition which was, in the end, both succinct and powerful - "Higher performance and profits in less time and with greater satisfaction – guaranteed." It brings him great returns.

What is your personal banner? Do you provide exceptional value for every client?

Jim Collins, in the book From Good to Great, suggests you create three circles and name them this way:

- What you can be the best in the world at?
- What drives your economic engine?
- What are you deeply passionate about?

This is no place to be modest. Define your brilliance and your passion and fit that into the marketplace.

So instead of asking 'What are the hot topics?' ask 'What do I have expertise in and how do I fit that into the marketplace?' and 'What message of value do I have?' Much better questions!

What is it you're brilliant at? What can you be best in the world at?

What areas are you weak in?

Where's the money?

What are you deeply passionate about?

How do your brilliance and passion intersect with the marketplace?

As you answer these questions, you may find that you need to completely revamp your current marketing strategy to achieve your best success.

Shine a bright light on yourself and look at the shadows as well as the brilliance. It's only then that you'll really move into your sphere. It's waiting for you. It's already in place.

Becoming a six-figure speaker is all about measurement of the satisfaction and the financial returns you are currently getting. Do you want to shift the balance of where your income currently comes from so that more income is generated by keynotes than training? What plan can you put in place to make that happen? How can you reposition yourself as a motivational speaker, for example, instead of as a trainer, while still maintaining and even growing your income base?

What are you leaving on the table? How can you gather it up? What kinds of opportunities have you been blind to? What added-value services can you add to serve your clients and boost your income? The speakers who succeed see opportunities that others are blind to.

It's alarming how many speakers go out there with a vision riding on a wing and a prayer – and not much else.

A vision is clearly something you need in your toolkit – but that's just a beginning. How do you plan to put it into place? How can you bring it in for a landing?

Some visions are grounded in practical wisdom while others are simply fantasies and ego trips.

Create your vision and write it down. Now live with it for a few days, look at it again. Have you thought of everything you want to see in your future as a speaker? Have you covered every aspect? Take a hard critical look at your vision statement. Are you thinking big enough or are you being just too modest and unassuming? Tweak your statement until it perfectly reflects what you want to see and be in the next couple of years.

Your vision should be a stretch for you. It should take you out of your current comfort zone or you're not dreaming big enough. Go on, take a deep breath, expand your horizons, spread your wings and dream bigger.

Add a measuring tool and a timeline to it. When will you know you achieved your goal? How long do you think it will take?

Chris Widener's vision statement was to represent the next generation of great speakers. He took drastic steps to put his vision into place which you'll read about in Chapter 19.

Here's what my vision statement would look like if I were marketing myself as a professional speaker:

"I intend to join the ranks of the world's most successful and respected speakers/consultants. I will carefully study the most successful business models, strengthen my positioning statement and embark on a course of constant learning by reading, attending courses and listening to top speakers. I will build a great marketing team and delegate whatever possible. I will initially spend at least 50% of my time on marketing by meeting new clients, getting good press and building a referral base. I will achieve my goal of being one of the world's most successful speakers within a five year period. I will know I'm on my way to achieving my goal when I share a platform with a world renowned speaker and I'll know I've arrived when my speaking income hits the high six figure mark."

What will your career look like in five years time? In 10? Twenty? Draft that plan now and rework it over the next few months until it exactly represents what you envisioned. You may rework it in six months time but for the moment you have a solid gold plan and you now need to add action steps and a time frame. Armed with this plan, there is nothing holding you back.

Start wherever you are right now and begin to build a strong foundation that can hold your future and everything you've ever dreamed of. Take the time now to create your own vision statement – make that commitment to yourself.

My Personal Vision Statement

_____

_____

_____

_____

_____

_____

In the next 12 months, I intend to:

_____

_____

_____

_____

_____

My action steps are:

_____

_____

_____

_____

_____

_____

_____

Now print out your vision statement and read it over once a day. You'll modify and add to it as you begin achieving your goals. You'll be amazed at the results. Only those people who clarify and consistently go after their objectives meet them and even surpass them.

If your vision includes becoming a six-figure speaker within six months or six years, you start by carefully assessing exactly where you are right now.

How much have you earned in the past six months as a speaker?

What can you do to bring that income up to six-figures in a certain time period? What does that mean on a monthly basis? How many gigs would you need to get? And how would you get them?

What other income streams will you put into place in case the bottom falls out of the professional speaking industry? Think that won't happen? It might. September 11, 2001, hit the speaking industry hard. So did a brief SARS epidemic in certain cities around the world.

It's always a good idea to have a few income streams in case one becomes temporarily indisposed.

Plan a strategy to begin the career of your dreams. Make it concrete; make it measurable. And check it on a weekly basis at first to make sure you're on track.

After that? Once you're doing all you can to put your plan in place, let it go. If your desire and your dream are really lined up, things will happen that you hadn't even thought of.

A final word – this road has paths that are not clearly visible from the starting point. Don't get so focused on implementing your plan that you miss the wonderful serendipity that is certain to come your way.

Speaking of serendipity, it's time to hear from Donald Cooper. He is so familiar with serendipity, he calls himself The Accidental Speaker.

CHAPTER 3

The Accidental Speaker
with Donald Cooper, MBA, CSP, HoF.

"Doing isn't difficult. Deciding is."
Foster Hubbard
former Director of Napoleon Hill Academy

No one was more surprised than Donald Cooper when he was inducted in the Canadian Speaking Hall of Fame at the CAPS National Conference in 2003.

"It was a huge surprise," he says. "The most I'd ever hoped for was 'The Accidental Speaker' award."

Of course, there's no such category. But if there were, Donald would be an excellent candidate. For the first 50 years of his life he had a very definite plan never to go on stage and never to be a speaker.

Donald stuttered as a teenager and had short-term memory challenges. In fact, he was so shy that he didn't start dating until he was in his twenties. "When I was a camp counselor at 17", he says, "I had a three-line part in a play and even though I practiced and practiced my three lines, when I got on stage I froze in front of the whole camp.

"The star of the show, at age 13, knew his 300 lines and my three lines perfectly, so he fed me my lines, one at a time in a stage whisper that could be heard clear to the back of the hall. I repeated my three lines, ran off stage, out the door and hid in the woods where I made a solemn vow never to set foot on stage again. Ever!"

Four decades later, at the age of 50, Donald owned and ran an extraordinary women's clothing store in Markham, Ontario. Word of his innovative marketing strategies spread to other retailers around the world. One day Donald got a call from the organizer of the world's most important retail and advertising conference inviting him to come to Chicago to share his experience.

"They didn't pay speakers and I had to pay my own expenses, but they said it was an honor to be asked. So I said yes and hung up. A few

11

months later I went to Chicago with 21 slides in my pocket. I spoke to 1,400 people for 45 minutes and when I got back to Toronto, the phone wouldn't stop ringing. The constant phone calls were distracting me from running my business so I figured that the next time someone called to ask me to speak, I'd ask for money and they'd hang up!"

When the next call came, Donald confidently stated that his speaking fee was $200. He was sure they'd hang up on him but instead they booked him. So, for the next booking enquiry came, he quoted a fee of $400 ... and they booked him.

"Clearly, my strategy wasn't working" he says, "so I just continued to double my fee until I got to $6,000 and by then I didn't want them to go away."

Eventually, Donald and his wife had to decide between retailing and speaking. "I was traveling and speaking so much that my wife was left to run the business and it wasn't fair. Besides, speaking had no inventory, no overhead and was open when and where we chose it to be. We thought about that for about six seconds ... and we sold the store."

Over his 15 years as a speaker Donald has met many people whom he calls "speakers in search of a topic." "What I discovered quite accidentally," he says, "on a stage in Chicago, at the age of 50, was that there was a topic out there that was in search of a speaker. There was a way of viewing a business and customers and life that was crying out for someone to articulate it clearly and passionately."

When people ask Donald about how to become a six-figure speaker he asks them two simple questions. First, what do you know more about than anyone else in the world that anyone gives a damn about? And second, do you have a way with a lyric?

The questions that follow are: Do you have a way of communicating your business-changing or life-changing ideas that grabs people's minds and hearts and souls? Do you have a way of making your ideas memorable and actionable?

Donald finds that most of the speakers asking his advice can't answer yes to those questions.

For his unique approach to customers, business and life Donald has trademarked the term "Human Marketing®," a term that he fell into accidentally. One day a customer with two small children in tow commented that his store was so wonderful that it was the only place in the world that she could shop and feel like a human being. To which he replied, "Thank you. I guess it's just human marketing." He trademarked the term internationally.

"There are 25,000 speakers in the world ... but only one of us can speak about 'Human Marketing.'" he says.

To excel in the speaking business, Donald recommends that "First of all, you need to know more about something that matters than anyone else in your market. You need a message that's either life-changing or business-changing. Period. What else is there? Find a perspective on your message or an edge to it and communicate it in a fresh way that makes people say 'I never thought of it that way before.' Then you need to be entertaining. Sleeping people learn nothing, so our first job is to keep them awake and our second job is to tell them stuff. If we don't do our first job, our second job doesn't matter. Finally, we need to uplift people. We need to be encouragers!"

Two things set Donald Cooper apart in the marketplace: his bottom-line business content and his edgy delivery. "I ride the line where people are challenged to think and to grow and to change. The problem is that that line, where we really help people, is very close to the line where some folks are upset or turned off. Many speakers are afraid to take it to the edge in case they fall over onto that other line and somebody doesn't like them.

"The secret is to be so good at reading the audience at every minute of your presentation that you know exactly where the line is. And that line moves. It's about building a relationship with the audience. You can get away with stuff at the 40-minute mark that you couldn't get away with at the 10-minute mark. The relationship has grown and the line has moved. Pros get this and make it work for them. I'm tuned in to my audience and I fearlessly ride that line."

Donald's message often contains hard truths. "Nobody hires me to sing Kumbayah." he says. "But, in order to get audiences to embrace those hard truths, we need to touch their minds, their hearts and their funny bones. The shortest distance between two people is a laugh. People won't change unless we first get them stressed about the current state of affairs in their business or their life. So, first I put them on the hook.

"But you can't leave them on the hook ... that would be cruel. I give them concepts, processes, tools, simple doable things that they can implement to get where they need to be. Then   I follow up the speech with a free monthly E-Newsletter full of short articles and tips to help then implement and grow. I call them booster shots and we need those in both our business and personal lives."

Donald's speeches are not memorized or canned. He does tons of research by sitting down with management and chatting with people in the trenches. "I tour factories, visit stores and travel with sales people," he says. "I have over 4,800 PowerPoint slides in my library of material and I want to know which of my slides will be absolutely relevant for each audience. I create a different presentation every time, based on what that particular audience needs.

"It's all about outcomes. With my short-term memory challenge, when I'm on stage with a particular slide up on the screen, I literally have no idea what the next slide is going to be. I press the clicker, look over my shoulder, glance at the slide and immediately recall what to say. I can recall like anything; I just can't remember. We all have challenges ... just get on with it!"

Donald's message has evolved over the years as he continues to move himself into higher income brackets with his speeches ... and now coaching.

"I started speaking to retailers about customer service and there's a limit to the amount of money people will pay for that. Then I realized that customer service is really part of a much bigger marketing challenge so I evolved into speaking about innovative marketing in over 40 different industries.

"Then it became clear that most businesses defined themselves in a way that made them self-centered, customer-unfriendly and unprepared for change. This revelation led to creating transformational work in the field of vision, mission and the very purpose of a business that has brought me to speaking to CEOs, entrepreneurs and top management about creating a degree of clarity about their business that will inform, focus, challenge and inspire everyone on their team.

"Clients will pay a lot more money for that message than retailers are prepared to pay for a speech about customer service. It's been an incredible evolution ... I've just kept moving myself up the food chain. Now, CEOs are paying me 10-grand a day to tell them how to transform their business and their role in it."

This new direction has taken Donald's life to a whole new level and has led to more work at a higher fee ... and more travel to more interesting places.

"I'm now working with people who can actually change an organization. It's more intellectually stimulating and much more gratifying."

As a business speaker and now coach, Donald has the advantage of being both a world-class manufacturer and an award-winning retailer.

"People want to hear from those who have walked in shoes that are very much like theirs, people who have been in the trenches. Many business speakers have never run a business."

Donald's advice to speakers is to "Design a business model that works for your life. Do you want to work only in your home city and sleep in your own bed every night? Do you want to speak nationally or globally with all that that entails? Do you not want to work on weekends or on your Sabbath, whatever it is, for your own good reasons?

"How many presentations do you want and need to do in a year to pay the bills, and have a life? What's really important to you? Canada is not a huge economic market so I decided early on that I needed to speak in the USA, Europe and Australia to build a broad client base.

"Do you want to build a business that you can eventually sell? Do you want to hire other speakers to deliver your message or other trainers to implement your ideas? Or will you run lean with yourself, an assistant and a home office? I've intentionally chosen not to build an organization or create overhead."

Donald's strategy is to keep it simple, make money and invest it wisely so that when he wants to slow down, he'll be able to do that without suffering financially. "One of the great things about this business is that as long as you're relevant," he says, "you can cut back your number of engagements a little every year depending on how you feel and what else you want to do.

"Nobody actually cares how many speeches you do a year. They just want the one that you're doing for them today to be helpful. We're so blessed to be in a business where we can decide when, where and how often we do what we do. We don't have to let anyone into our lives that we don't want to and we don't have to work when we have other things we'd rather do.

"Tonight – New Year's Eve – my wife and I will decide how many engagements to aim for this year and next week, my assistant and I will develop a plan to achieve that goal. Sure we should have done that about three months ago … but we didn't and we'll get over it."

Most of Donald's work comes from repeat engagements and referrals. "As speakers we don't exactly do what we do in a closet with the lights out. We do it in front of thousands of people a year. So, the most effective marketing is to show up and be very, very good. Make a difference! Have the courage to tell the truth and the skill to tell it wonderfully. Be kind, be an encourager … and finish on time. That's about it."

Great guidelines for becoming an accidental or even an intentional speaker!

Find out more about Donald at www.donaldcooper.com.

CHAPTER 4

On Top of Time

"We first make our habits and then our habits make us."
John Dryden

In order to be a highly successfully speaker, you need to take a close look at your relationship with time. Are you making the best possible use of it? Or could you be more efficient?

You can't be successful without staying on top of your time. There's no other element, aside from attitude and energy, that has a more direct link to achievement. We all need to look at and constantly modify the way we manage our time. The people who achieve so much very effortlessly are simply masters at organizing and staying on top of their schedules.

Do you realize how much procrastination costs you in terms of productivity? What would it mean to you financially if you got more done in less time? Finish old projects or dump them. Take a weekend, or even a week if you need it, and clear the slate of the things that are holding you back or create a time frame to get them done and stick to it. Unfinished projects take a lot of energy.

Clean up your messes. They hold you back much more than you realize.

Most speakers realize very quickly that they spend a small percentage of their time actually speaking and devote a huge amount of time to marketing.

This will be true for you too. Most of your time needs to be spent in highly productive and income-generating activities, such as marketing or product development and under product development I include developing a new speech or training program.

As one of the world's top copywriters, Bob Bly's time-management principles apply as easily to speakers as to writers since both occupations involve a lot of time spent just managing projects.

If you have a good marketing campaign going, you'll be working

16

on short-term and long-term projects such as books, mailing lists, database updates, web updates, new speeches, press releases, marketing initiatives, etc. It can be tricky to stay on top of it all.

Bly's advice is to break your day into segments and write down the project you will work on during each of those segments. He says, "Do this every day at the beginning of your workday. Tape your hour-by-hour schedule for the day on a wall near your desk, or pin it to a nearby bulletin board.

"As you go through your day, consult your schedule to keep on track. If priorities change, you can change the schedule, but do this in writing. Revise the schedule, print the new version, remove the old schedule and post the new one."

Bly is so fond of lists that he even posts a list that he updates weekly called Rules of the Office. His number one rule is First Things First – it reminds him to keep an eye on his bottom line by setting priorities and meeting deadlines.

"For instance," says Bly, "if I am burning to work on a book but have a press release due the next morning, I write the press release first and fax or e-mail it to the client. Then I reward myself with a morning spent on the book. If you do the book first, you may not leave yourself enough time to get the press release written by your deadline."

Wise advice!

The super-organized Bly keeps three lists.

Every morning, after checking for e-mail, he opens his LISTS file; it tells him which lists he must read and review to start his day.

"The most important lists on the LISTS list are my to-do lists," Bly claims. "I keep several, but the most critical are my daily to-do list, projects to-do lists and long-term to-do list:

"1. Daily to-do list. Each day I type, print and post a list of the items I have to do that day. From this list, I create my hour-by-hour schedule. I never take on more than I can handle so I can continue to meet all deadlines.

"2. Projects to-do list. In a separate computer file, I keep a list of all my writing projects currently under contract, along with the deadline for each. I review this list several times a week, using it to ensure that the daily to-do list covers all items that have to be done right away.

"3. Long term to-do list. This is a list of projects I want to do at some point but are not under contract (such as learning new software or organizing files) and therefore do not have any assigned deadlines. I check this list about once a week and usually put in a few hours each week on one or two of the projects that interest me at the time.

"Having a daily to-do list – and assigning various tasks to yourself throughout the day in one-hour increments – helps you stay on track and avoid putting things off."

Bly feels that the best way to make every hour of every day

productive is to have an hour-by-hour schedule. "People who have such a schedule know what they should be doing every minute, and therefore do it. People who don't set a schedule tend to drift through the day, stopping and then starting tasks, jumping from job to job without getting much done."

Bly's organizational skills have contributed to his phenomenal success. Adopt and adapt his principles to your speaking career.

It will take you some time to set this up but it will pay off in spades.

- What's immediate for you?
- What's critical?
- What's more of a long-term project?
- What are the things you know you need to do that don't have a strict deadline? Fit them into your schedule or they won't happen.

Make sure the main focus of your attention is on income-generating activities. As you determine priorities, keep cash flow issues in view by always asking yourself "What's fueling my economic engine?"

A book project, for example, needs a separate list of things you need to do to finish and promote the book which will fit into your every day to-do list. Yet a book project may not immediately generate income so you have to find time for it without detracting from your money-making projects. Personally, I think Bly's advice to have more than one list is very astute.

Make sure that your priority time is spent on income-generating activities.

And here's something that will strike a chord with all of us.

Ever heard of time vampires? You know those folks who call you in the middle of the workday just to chat, the same people who feel that you don't have a "real" job.

According to Dan Kennedy, author of the No B.S. Time Management for Entrepreneurs, time vampires are the people who would happily steal your time. He recommends that you become highly skilled in spotting them and "driving stakes through their hearts".

"People and activities that drain your energy are the greatest time thieves of all," he says. "Fire clients that you don't have a great relationship with, create a distance with friends or colleagues who leave you feeling drained and straighten out a relationship where there's conflict. That will do more to free up your time than any kind of super efficiency exercise.

"In other words, be ruthless with your time."

Kennedy also recommends that you calculate exactly what your time is worth in order to make good time decisions. If you're aiming for $600,000 annually, estimate how much of your time is directly billable and how much of it is involved in supporting activities, such as mailing out promotional packages, making phone calls, etc. Billable hours are those hours where you're actually getting paid for your work. For speakers, billable hours are the hours spent delivering a keynote speech or doing training or consulting work.

Increase the billable hours and hire someone to do the mailing and phoning.

How much of your time converts into billable hours and how much is devoted to support activities?

Calculating that bottom-line figure helps you know exactly what your time per hour is worth and also keeps your finger on the pulse of your income-generating activities.

There are 244 work days in a year and, at eight hours a day, 1,952 hours a year. For professional speakers, few of those hours will be directly billable. Most hours will be spent marketing, networking and upgrading information and skills.

Make sure those activities are as productive and as closely related to direct income-generation as possible.

Here are some questions for you – think hard and long about the answers - they can completely transform your approach to your speaking career.

- What's your time worth per hour?
- How are you spending it?
- How can you increase the number of billable hours?
- What (and who) do you need to let go of?
- Can you manage your schedule more efficiently?
- What can you delegate?
- Do you avoid time-wasting meetings, e-mails, phone calls, etc.?
- If you take on a new project, do you cut back on something else?
- Do you find if you have a little extra time on your hands that you'll take on something new rather than polish off some outstanding projects?
- Can you stretch yourself in terms of time while still maintaining a high degree of energy, health and joy?
- Who are your time vampires and how can you handle them?
- What are your time-wasters and how can you reduce them? (Distinguish between a time-waster and something that's relaxing.)

And make sure you're having fun in what you're doing. Don't get grim about time management but do be ruthless in allocation. It's worth it – so are you!

CHAPTER 5

Scaling the Heights
with Rich Fettke

"Out of need springs desire and out of desire springs the energy and the will to win."

Denis Waitley

Rich Fettke, author of Extreme Success, will never forget the day he went to New York with his agent. On their first day in New York city, they met with six publishers and on their second day, they met with two.

Rich is from Northern California and is used to wide open spaces, so he was struck by the towering building that belonged to Simon & Schuster, one of the publishers they met with on the second day. It was February 23, 2000, and it was Rich's birthday. Both he and his agent felt the meeting went well and were prepared for the waiting game.

They hired a limo to take them to the hotel when his agent's cell phone rang.

It was Simon & Schuster saying, "Please don't accept any offers until you've considered ours." That was not a problem. Simon and Schuster made a six-figure offer that Rich was thrilled with. Very well done for a new author!

Rich's book proposal was originally called "The Power of Partnership" and he couldn't get a nibble from publishers. When he changed the title to Extreme Success and added stories of his exploits as an adventure athlete, the book became much more marketable.

Getting an offer from Simon & Schuster was Rich's highest moment in the speaking/writing/training business. Life being cyclical, he's had extreme lows as well. That's simply the nature of the business.

Along with many other speakers, getting into the field of professional speaking just naturally evolved.

"I owned a large health club franchise in the Boston area," he says, "and the biggest challenge was getting clients to stay motivated with their fitness programs. So I started going to schools and local groups and Rotaries, speaking about motivation for fitness. I then started a personal fitness training company in California and began to speak about motivation there as well. My speech naturally evolved into 'What is it that motivates people to do what's best for them' ... whether it's fitness or finance or whatever?"

It was a large question that took Rich down some very interesting paths.

"I began to get more training in business and in personal coaching. I got certified by the Coaches Training Institute which led to more media exposure as I served on the board and also as president of the country's largest coaching association. That was a big part of the puzzle."

When Rich started out speaking in 1990, he didn't charge anything. His first fee-based engagement was in 1996 in California. He charged $200. "That felt about right then," he says. "My focus was on coaching for the first few years, building my coaching business, coaching clients and taking information and weaving it into an online newsletter, creating a book proposal and so on."

Although he was very good at his speeches, speaking engagements did not fall from the sky. "Lots of people have the fantasy that once you call yourself a speaker you start getting bookings, but for me, not much was happening. I wasn't letting people know that I gave speeches or contacting associations or corporations since I didn't have to do that with coaching. It was easy getting coaching clients. I'd simply introduce myself, go to networking events and build my business from referrals and the whole media thing."

"Once the book came out in June 2002 it became my major focus. I started to do a lot more radio and television and not too long ago, I hired a woman to contact groups that would be a good fit. That was a big lesson. I learned that no one can sell you like you can – but also no one can sell you like someone else can. You need to both make calls yourself and delegate calls to a staff member.

"Here's the distinction. Doing the initial contacts calls – the cold-calls – personally, where I was looking for the right fit and asking 'Do you hire speakers? Who have you hired in the past? What do you look for in a speaker?', was ineffective. People wondered why I made the calls myself.

"Yet seeds need to continually be planted. Someone had to make those calls. Six months ago, I hired a woman to only do that. I do the follow-up. It's working great. Where before, I'd send out a couple of packages a week, now we're sending out 10 info packages a week, with video, a copy of my book and a promo package."

Rich's career took a significant leap forward once he got a contract with a major publisher. "It's a great goal to strive for. I was out rock-climbing with a partner. I said you know what – I've got enough feedback from people to justify doubling my fee to $5,000. No one blinked at it – it was a real light-bulb moment. Whenever I raised my fee as coach, within that week I'd get new clients at my new fee."

From his experience, Rich has sage advice for speakers. "Don't wait until you're ready. Don't wait until you're comfortable. If you're comfortable with your fee, it's probably too low."

Rich usually does three or four speeches a month and he still does the coaching, working with 10 clients a month. He's gradually moving towards increasing his speaking fee and decreasing the number of coaching clients.

He feels that success comes from "bringing who you are to your speaking. There are so many speakers out there trying to copy the top speakers. Newer speakers try to be everything to everybody. All they can be is themselves. When I started to be who I am and brought adventure sports and videos into my presentations, my speaking career began to take off."

"As a speaker, I shifted my focus to taking action because it's what makes me unique. I was diagnosed with ADD when I was young, now I've flipped that around and made staying focused and creating action my expertise. It's been really powerful.

"What's unique about you and your story? What are you known for? What do people who associate with you say about you? Bring that to your marketing and to the platform.

"Speak as much as possible in the early years; take on those speaking engagements even at less than full fee that meet a certain criteria for you, such as meeting planners in the audience or being videotaped. Let people see your stuff. It doesn't matter how great you are, if people don't know you're there nothing will happen."

Rich is on NBC 11 twice a year and recently did an interview on focusing for the New Year. Having his book published brought him many media appearances. While on a book tour in 2002, Rich had so many opportunities fall into his lap that he was on a real high. Once the tour ended, he "started to dip down." Engagements weren't coming in so rapidly and then came a huge blow. Rich was diagnosed with melanoma.

"Doctors thought it had spread to my liver," he says, "and I went through two months not knowing whether I'd live or not. It was really a time of reassessment for me – was I doing what I really wanted to do or not?"

The answer wasn't all that long in coming. "One of the life's greatest thrills" says this extreme adventurer "is being on the platform. There's an energy there that's kind of like bungee jumping but even better. There's something about the energy exchange between you and the audience. I'm laughing, they're laughing and yet what we're talking about is meaningful and important. I love it!"

Rich's most gratifying speaking engagement was when he spoke to the American Marketing Association at Walt Disney's World Resort.

"It was a great group of 1,700 enthusiastic people. It was just one of those moments where I felt a really great connection. It was full of fun, we were laughing, there was applause after my stories, and of course, the venue was beautiful with two Imax screens on each side of me so everyone could see my videos as I spoke."

Engagements like that make it all worthwhile.

Rich's goals for the future are to continue to raise his fee and consistently speak four times a month. Also "finding, connecting and speaking for groups that are the best fit; people who are responsible for their own business development and who need to be self-directed and self-motivated. These are the people I'd love to reach – business owners and sales people."

Rich can be reached at www.fettke.com

CHAPTER 6

Don't Leave Home Without It
The One Essential Marketing Tool

"We are all salespeople, every day of our lives. We are selling our ideas, our plans, our enthusiasms to those with whom we come in contact."

Charles Schwab, former CEO Bethlehem Steel

It continues to amaze me that some of the world's top speakers don't have this critical marketing tool. It's not difficult or expensive to design or produce and is really an essential marketing tool.

I'm talking about the one-pager. It's a single sheet of paper that lists your qualifications, your topics, a list of your clients and testimonials.

How simple is that?

You NEED this one-pager. Otherwise, you'll handicap your staff and your work with bureaus.

As a bureau owner, I can tell my clients that you're a great speaker but I need corroborative evidence. I need to prove my point. That's what the one-pager helps to do. No-one who pays for your services as a speaker is willing to take a bureau's word for it unless they can back it up.

You may get most of your gigs by word-of-mouth referrals and that's great. However, imagine what you could do and all the people you could reach if you were more proactive. You'd cast a much wider net.

At Speakers Gold, we won't take on any speaker, no matter how accomplished, without great marketing materials. Why? Because these speakers are too hard for a third party to sell.

Here's what goes into a one-pager:

- Bio
- Personal logo or mission statement
- Photo
- Three speech titles (more or less)

- Blurbs about each speech
- Client List
- Testimonials

Let's consider the text first because the truth is COPY IS KING! Your design might be state of the art but if you don't have compelling text on your one-pager, you might as well pack up your tent and crawl away.

Start by planning your positioning in the market place. That begins with your name or company name. I recommend going with only your name since, unless you're well-known or your branding is very consistent, it's confusing to throw three things at your prospective client, i.e. your name, your company name and the name of your keynote. So my advice is to stick with your name.

For example, if I wanted to position myself as a keynote speaker, it might look like this:

> Speakers Gold
> Cathleen Fillmore
> Speech: 'Mindset for the Millennium'

If I'm unknown to the buyer, that's a lot to remember. I'd be better off going with just my name and keynote title since it's less confusing. You don't want to put obstacles of any sort in front of your buyer.

Once you're well-known, you can use all three. For example, Jim Ruta, a platform speaker at the Million Dollar Round Table in 2007, uses this:

> The Expert Institute
> Jim Ruta
> Speech: 'Crack the Code'

Jim's well known in financial service circles and his branding is completely consistent.

It works well.

You need a great photo on your one-pager. It should be an excellent enhanced natural photo – nothing contrived.

Find the right photographer to provide the perfect balance between a natural shot and something so fake that people faint when they meet you in person. We're looking for inner beauty here not a facsimile of the real you.

Please be natural in your poses. No jumping in the air, no dramatic postures, just allow your own naturally beautiful self to shine through. The right photographer can capture that essence and broadcast it out to the world.

A full body shot is really compelling. You look so authoritative, so much in command and in your power. If you have a two-sided one-pager, I recommend a head shot on one side and on the other side, a full body shot of you just standing naturally.

To see some wonderful promo photos, go to www.susansweeney.com.

Lance Secretan has a great photo of his dog licking his face on his website. It's a compelling shot and shows who Lance really is. Check it out at www.secretan.com. Be careful with this pose, though. Unless you've reached the stature of Alan Weiss or Lance Secretan, a photo of you with your dog will just brand you as an amateur. Once you've established your branding as a serious credible speaker with a great corporate client list, you can break the same rules that you adhered to when you started out.

Your bio should be well-written in a way that captures the reader's interest. Check out the NSA and CAPS websites to read other speaker's bios. Don't be too wordy here. Make each word carry its own weight. Is that word really needed? If not, toss it. Remember that your prospective clients really are more interested in what you can do for them than in who you are.

Now let's talk about topics. You need topics that catch the client's interest. Adventurer Martyn Williams has a wonderful photo of himself climbing Mount Everest with his beard covered in ice.

But the name of his topic was originally a little lame, something like 'Climbing the Mountain'. Just too prosaic! So we brainstormed and came up with 'In the Eye of a Storm: How Leaders Face a Crisis'. That was perfect. All we did was look at his photo and translate that into words. Now his photo and his topic were equally compelling. A perfect match.

Let's measure the title 'In the Eye of a Storm' by my criteria.

- The words need to be melodic, they should flow.
- They need to create a visual image.
- Preferably conjure up a heroic image.
- They need to be easy to say and remember.

'In the Eye of a Storm' passes with flying colors. Melodic, easy to remember, creates a visual image and the reader immediately feels a little like a hero just by listening to this speech. Who hasn't been in the eye of some kind of storm? Who doesn't want to feel like a hero?

While the speech content hasn't changed, Martyn's speech is now much easier to market and sell. Keep in mind that your buyer needs to feel an emotional attachment to your topic in order to book you. Then he or she will need to justify that booking logically so your written material should address both these needs.

Here are a few things to consider when writing the text for your marketing materials. The English language is composed of five languages. Avoid Latin-based words in your title. That was the language the aristocracy used centuries ago and today those words sound academic rather than conversational, approachable and friendly.

Words such as 'institution', 'economic' and 'financial' tend to lie flat on the page. They're dead words. You want your words to be so vivid they jump right off the page into the reader's heart and mind. In other words, you want your words to convey how vivid and lively you are.

Centuries ago, the common people used a mix of German and Anglo-Saxon. It's from that base that we get most of our colorful idioms. This is the spoken language we tend to use in conversation today and it's what I recommend you rely on as a foundation for all of your written material, particularly your titles.

Think of your own great title. It's often right under your nose. Visit bookstores and pick out the titles that you find appealing. Which books do you reach out for? Which titles do you get a pleasant physical reaction to? Which ones are repellent? Focus on finding the perfect title for your topic and sooner or later it will come to you.

Your title doesn't have to be crystal clear, it's sometimes good to raise a question in the buyer's mind, as long as the subtitle clarifies. Here's the formula: appealing visual image and melodic words for the title and absolute clarity for the subtitle.

Author and speaker Ezell Ware's book has a brilliant title: By Duty Bound: Survival and Redemption in Vietnam. Very compelling. The subtitle clarifies the topic. Compelling book, too, by the way. You'll find it listed in the recommended reading material.

Here's the way professional speaker Robin Kennedy named two of her speeches:

1. Class Act: Build Ironclad Credibility in a World Searching for People & Companies to Trust.
2. Lead by Following: Create a Deeper Connection with Employees, Customers & Stakeholders.

Excellent titles. Are your topics as compelling as possible? Can you take them up a notch?

The late E. Haldeman-Julius said that finding the perfect title was nothing less than genius. He proved himself right by selling more than 100 million books during the first part of the twentieth century. His book The First Hundred Million gives a rare glimpse into the power of just the right title.

Haledeman-Julius left nothing to chance. He tested his titles by simply advertising his list of books by title alone in a newspaper or magazine ad. He listed nothing else, only the title of the book. That was it.

When a title failed to sell over 10,000 copies annually, it was sent to a place in his office called "The Hospital" and, in most cases, a new title was found. One of his books was called the Art of Controversy which never really sold, until it was changed to How to Argue Logically when suddenly it sold 30,000 copies. Same content, only the title changed. It made all the difference.

Haldeman-Julius found that title words could increase the sales of almost any book. For instance, the words "The Truth About" added to a book title increased sales from 3,000 to 10,000. The words "The Truth About" are compelling even today.

The words "How to" added to a title invariably boosted sales and "The Facts You Should Know" also proved to be a winning prefix to a title.

How can you apply this brilliant man's research to your positioning statement and titles?

You're the Expert

Position yourself as the solution-provider, the expert, rather than the speaker. What problems do you solve? What is your positioning statement? What can you do for the buyer? He or she cares about that more than anything, more than your credentials, more than your client list. How can you help them?

I've found that the easiest way to sell your speech is to tie what you're doing to the bottom line. Is that because we're just a money-mad society and only financial gains have meaning? Not at all. It's got more to do with buyers wanting a solid measurable return on their investment in you. And an increase in revenues is a solid benefit that is quantifiable. It's easy to measure.

If you're offering team-building or customer service or enthusiasm in the workplace or even humor, tie it to the bottom line. Make that equation for your client in case she doesn't make it herself. Make it a no-brainer.

How about - "Robert works with companies that want to dramatically increase their revenues." (Note that Robert says 'works with' rather than 'helps' which is kind of patronizing.)

Gee, Robert, how do you do that? Will you show me how to rob a bank? Get involved in shady deals?

"Well, no, actually. Our stats show clearly that companies that take action on boosting employee morale consistently report a dramatic increase in revenues and soar ahead of their competitors."

Works for me!

Back to Paul Lemberg. "Higher performance and profits in less time and with greater satisfaction – guaranteed." That brief elevator speech is a great marketing tool.

Create an amazingly polished positioning statement for yourself. Once you've determined your topics, write a blurb about them that focuses on your audience's needs. Many speakers do this in bullet points.

How will listening to this speech benefit someone in the audience? More importantly, how will this speech benefit the person signing your check?

Take a moment to read your title and your description of your speech. If someone else were delivering this speech, would you go out on a cold night after work to hear it? If the honest answer is no, then it's back to the drawing board.

If you're not super excited about your topic, no one else will be either.

Robin Kennedy's benefits for Class Act are:

- Establish rapport quickly
- Facilitate candid conversations
- Uncover the real issues

How will your speech affect the person in the audience? And how will this benefit the company or association that hired you? What value will last once you've left the room? These are your bullet benefits and they're a powerful component of your one-pager.

Now add your client list. If you have fewer than 10 clients, I'd advise you to leave them off for now and instead substitute great testimonials from the few clients you've spoken to.

Add testimonials from those who've heard you speak. Whether your speech was no-fee or well-paid, the testimonials are just as valid. Lead with your strongest ones and you can edit a little and also correct any grammatical irregularities. When appropriate, use a great testimonial as a banner on your website and marketing materials.

You'll find that your well-designed one-pager, printed on high quality paper is the most useful and cost effective marketing tool of all. Quality paper. Not recycled paper. Not printed off your computer (unless you're a talented designer). You yourself are a class act, your material needs to reflect that.

Don't print too many copies. The strongest marketing tactic is to send out the PDF version of your material when requested, follow up by mailing a hard copy. You only want a minimum of hard copies on hand since your material will need to be updated regularly.

While some speakers may do okay by presenting customized proposals to their clients, the truth is that if you don't have stand-alone marketing materials that market on your behalf, you're hurting yourself by not being able to extend your reach beyond your own community.

You're limiting your growth.

YOU are not a commodity. Your speeches, however, are. So are your training programs. They're a product and if they're not well defined, they'll be a tough sell.

You'll reinvent the wheel if you have to develop completely customized programs at fluctuating prices for each of your prospective clients. You'll also damage your credibility. The speaking world is a small one and people talk. If you gave a program for one bank at a certain fee and yet charged another bank less for basically the same program, you will get caught sooner or later. Be consistent with your programs and your prices.

I trust I've made my case for a one-pager and having a well-developed menu of services (if you offer more than keynotes) which you will then customize to meet the buyer's objectives.

To recap, your one-pager should consist of your bio, your speeches, bullet benefits, a client list, testimonials and a great photo. It needs to be updated regularly.

Leave off the fees, those can be discussed by phone or e-mail.

Creating a brilliantly designed and written one-pager is the one essential marketing tool you can't do without. How would you rate yours? How can you take it to the next level? Is it time for a revamp or maybe even a complete new branding process?

Regularly review your one-pager to see if it needs modifying.

Postcard Campaigns

Another brilliant and low cost marketing tool is the postcard. Postcards can bring you excellent returns when you use them strategically.

Alexandria Brown, the e-zine queen, was skeptical when someone suggested that mailing postcards is a great way to build business. All her business is done online and she thought mail-outs were antiquated. However, she gave it a try. She sent out postcards to all the clients who hadn't yet signed up for her intensive mentoring program. She got such a great return that postcards have become part of her overall marketing strategy ever since.

When Internet marketer Alex Mandossian began using postcard marketing for dental products he was promoting, he was stunned by the huge return on investment he got back. So much so that he moved to New York City and became the Postcard King of Information Marketing.

"I love postcards," Mandossian says. "They're the fastest, easiest, most economical way to increase sales and profits without spending an extra dime on sales and advertising and the recipient gets to see the message right there. I found it worked better than e-mail – there's never a virus attached to it and you can't delete it forever. Postcards are an overlooked marketing secret and, if taken seriously, can be very profitable to any business."

Mandossian met a cartoonist in a wheelchair who sold his work by going door to door. Alex showed him how to put his art on a postcard. With one mail drop, the cartoonist reached 250 people at once and his business exploded – without expending a lot of money or time.

One success coach Mandossian worked with mailed out 1,200 postcards four times and picked up eight new clients in about 60 days – all worth about $3,000 each.

As a marketing tactic, postcards can work very well for professional speakers. You can use them to invite bureaus or prospective clients to come hear you speak. Postcards are also a great way of announcing a new book release or letting clients know that you've just gotten your CSP designation.

You can also send out postcards two weeks in advance of a tradeshow where you'll be speaking.

With his postcard marketing campaigns, Mandossian uses the PAR Formula. Problem, Action, Results. First define the problem. Then decide what action would be most effective, using principles, tactics and techniques to solve that problem. R stands for results – what results do you expect from this action?

What Alexandria Brown used to great effectiveness was a postcard that featured a picture of her cat and herself. The message was "Francine and I are looking for you." Then she goes on to say "Did we miss something? We have not seen YOUR registration for our Online Success Blueprint Workshop yet. We urge you not to wait any longer to reserve your spot because we already 67% solid out. So turn this card over and get your ticket today."

Very effective. The photo of Alexandria and her cat added a personal touch.

Let's say your problem is that you want to reach an entirely new group of clients in a country where you're not known. You decide on the following action. You compile a mailing list, create a postcard with a powerful message and call to action which might be requesting more information or setting up a phone appointment.

To maximize your results, Mandossian suggests you consider the following three principles:

1. Frequency is the best way to capture more sales.

Think of it – your best friend was once a stranger. And the only thing that made that person your best friend was the frequency with which you communicated with him or her. Frequency builds trust.

It's much better to mail a thousand targeted prospects four times than one postcard to 4,000 prospects. Frequency is superior to "reach". Familiarity breeds trust in postcard marketing, not contempt. Because your postcard is an unexpected guest, the more often they see it, the better.

Unless you can afford to mail at least four postcards to the same list, don't bother. One postcard does not make a campaign. Mandossian sent out 1,200 postcards and got a 28% response of people who wanted to talk to him. That's a great response. And he eliminated people who weren't interested. That's also important.

2. Mailing Lists

Mailing lists predetermine success or failure.

Without a great mailing list, your postcard is useless. People have different ideas about the importance of the offer, the price and the call to action, as well as the copy and design and mailing list. Here's what you need to keep in mind.

"The mailing list is 70% of your success, copy and design are only 10%," says Mandossian. "Then the offer is 20%. Spend your time focusing on finding the best mailing list."

3. Use only one of the two postcard copywriting formats.

There are two types of formats in writing copy. One three-step formula is:

- Make a promise.
- Give reasons why this promise is to be proved.
- Call to Action – get them to do something.

The second model is the Dale Carnegie model.

- Tell a memorable story.
- Give the Call to Action.
- Name the benefits they'll gain by taking that action.

Both are effective. You need to conduct a market test to see which approach works best with your target market.

If you use these three principles – frequency, an excellent mailing list and a compelling message (which can be a very simple one) – and combine them with a great postcard design, you will get an excellent return-on-investment on your postcard campaign. (Alex Mandossian can be reached at www.alexmandossian.com)

An outstanding one-pager combined with a strategic use of postcards will be the most effective marketing tools you've got in your toolkit.

I rest my case!

CHAPTER 7

The Client as Royalty
No Prima Donnas, Please!

"I was but a bad speaker, never eloquent, subject to much hesitation in my choice of words, hardly correct in language and yet I generally carried my point."

Benjamin Franklin

Do you leave your clients wanting more? Do they reap enormous benefits from your advice and refer you to others? That's the kind of atmosphere you want to create in order to build a solid reputation and speaking business. Some speakers rely on referrals alone to build their business.

It's important for your clients and audiences to value you.

So let's start with what not to do. When I interviewed meeting planners and bureaus across North America, many said that they didn't appreciate speakers who had an inflated sense of their own importance. The refrain was "No prima donnas, please!"

Prima donnas flourished a few years ago.

We all remember the speaker who arrived just before the conference and flounced in breathless a few minutes before he or she had to speak. The one who didn't bother to let anyone know he'd arrived and then after the speech, swept out with his entourage.   And hit the client with a big fat bill for expenses after the event.

Those speakers have had their day and those days are gone!

Meeting planners know that this type of speaker's time in the spotlight is over because they, like many others, are learning to steer away from the "big names" – especially those without a solid message – and instead book speakers who may not have such a high profile but who are willing to go the extra mile. Speakers who leave behind value for the client. Speakers who not only shine on the platform but offer incentives that make the bureau or conference organizer look good in their client's

eyes.

'No prima donnas need apply," says Sarah Fitting, Product Development Specialist with Bravo Meeting Management Solutions in Toronto, Ontario. "We don't want to work with them." Sarah has discovered that, all too often with high-profile speakers, "You have to manage the speaker as well as the client – and that creates extra work and expenses. You're already worrying about 400 delegates and then have to spend time making complicated travel arrangements for the speaker."

Every meeting planner has a story. Sarah's most bizarre incident involved a speaker whose fee was not commensurate with market demand, yet he insisted that his entourage of 8 to 10 extra people travel with him. "Needless to say, he didn't get the booking!"

Cass Bayley, of The Bayley Group in Hensall, Ontario, agrees with Sarah. She's personally seen three or four big names go flat with the audience. "Maybe it's an issue of high expectations," she comments. "Personally, I'd rather find an unknown than go with a big name unless I really have to."

"We find the bigger the name, the less likely the speaker is to tailor their talk to the client and a lack of customizing can erode the whole meeting. There's a domino effect," says Sarah Fitting.

Prima donnas are not the only issue for meeting planners. There are other things speakers sometimes do that really annoy the bureau or conference organizer who booked them.

Cass Bayley's worst case scenarios have involved speakers who ramble, go over time or arrive late or in a bad mood. "I've had a speaker drive into the hotel driveway as I'm calling his cell phone with two minutes to spare. I've also seen big names give a speech with no recognition of the audience or any attempt to connect with audience members."

Cass also says that she avoids speakers who deliver a canned presentation that hasn't been molded to fit the audience.

Sarah Fitting has another issue with speakers. "What we don't like is when speakers contact our clients directly without checking that out with us first. If a speaker wants to talk about agenda or goals, they should filter that through us first."

In other words, if you're booked through a third-party agency, don't contact the client directly unless instructed to do so by the agency.

"Another big issue," says Sarah, "is that we educate our clients that we don't pay a bureau, instead the speaker pays commission. Speakers working with bureaus need to watch that they're not undercutting bureaus by going direct. The speaking world is a small world. Everyone talks."

Cass Bayley has this advice for speakers who try to fit into all molds. "It's important to be honest with people. Don't sell yourself for senior-level management when you're not at that level and then go in with entry-level ideas. Unless you have a new message or a book, it's hard to impress people at a senior level. If you don't have a cutting-edge message, keep your day job. Know your audience and your level and be honest about that. The meeting-planning industry is small enough that word gets around pretty quickly about who's easy to work with and who bombed onstage. Word-of-mouth is always the most reliable way of lowering the risk of hiring the wrong speaker for the event."

What Sarah looks for is a speaker who's willing to simplify travel requirements and expenses. "We prefer to pay a flat fee for the speaker's travel and to take care of the bookings ourselves. As part of a travel-management company, it's easier for us to incorporate travel arrangements for the speaker. The speakers who simplify their requirements and are succinct about them are easy to deal with and make our lives easier."

As for customization, Sarah talks about a meeting with a travel-related theme of team-building. "The speaker took a stock talk and tailored it to include the buzz words, catch phrases and pertinent issues in the travel industry. It went over amazingly well. It seems basic but it doesn't always happen."

Her final word of advice to speakers is, "Be on time. And don't arrive frazzled. It's always helpful if we can get a copy of your presentation ahead of time and also if you inform us whether you need audiovisual equipment."

The Bayley Group looks for speakers who are creative, custom-design their presentation for audiences and stick to their time allotment.

"Conferences have extremely tight schedules" says Cass, "so going over time is not an option. Most are sensitive to the audience and can tell when it goes on too long. As a last resort, we ask the speaker to keep it snappy."

The speaker and meeting planner have to brief each other well and the speaker should have all possible information beforehand. "Speakers who ask for more conference information impress me," Cass claims. "I also appreciate it when speakers are flexible with their fee. We work with a range of high-end corporate functions to tight-budgeted associations as well as not-for-profit organizations. They all have different audiences and different budgets. Bureaus will also help us cut our costs and tell us when a particular speaker is in town so we save on travel cost."

Meeting planners and bureaus agree that speakers at the $5,000 fee need a video and references. Companies are not willing to invest $5,000 unless they can see your platform skills for themselves. Lots of speakers look good on paper yet don't do so well on the platform.

Make your audience feel you're connecting with them individually. Convey enthusiasm, passion and high energy. Know what you're talking about, connect with your passion and be articulate in your delivery. Care about your audience. That means forgetting about any feelings of self-consciousness.

You want the audience members to leave feeling special and have people discussing your speech and asking questions. You want people going out with a feeling that their time has been well spent. Meeting planners are always looking for great speakers and are also quick to spread the word if someone is a disappointment.

It's clear why Kit Grant, CSP, is such a popular speaker.

"I'm low maintenance," he claims. "I don't ask to be picked up at the airport, I fly coach and I don't drink. My AV is minimal and I always ask what I can do to help make the meeting planner's job easier. Meeting planners also appreciate the fact that I'll do both a breakout session and a keynote for the same fee. I will adjust my speech if the program's running late or fill in if there's a no-show."

Another speaker who exceeds meeting planners' expectations is Eli Bay. A pioneer in the field of stress relief, Eli really walks his talk when working with meeting planners.

"True to my topic," he says, "I make their lives as stress-free as possible. It's my policy to arrive well in advance of the event and to let the planner know immediately that I'm there. In cases where I arrive the night before, I also offer a deep relaxation session for the organizers of the conference so they're relaxed and refreshed the day of the event." The importance of being relaxed can't be over-emphasized, he claims. "There are always last-minute challenges and a relaxed de-stressed meeting planner is better able to deal with them. It really can mean the difference between a successful or unsuccessful event."

Meeting planners are also often asked to recommend a speaker for a conference they're organizing. While they don't take commissions on the speaker's fee, they, like bureaus, put their reputation on the line every time they recommend a speaker.

"While meeting planners are always looking for good speakers," says Cass Bayley of The Bayley Group, "we're also quick to spread the word if a speaker is disappointing." The meeting planning circuit is a relatively small one and word – whether good or bad – travels at lightning speed.

Hiring a speaker who's not right for the event is much less likely to happen when the planner gets a referral from a speaker's bureau.

"We work closely with several reputable speaking agencies that we have learned to trust over the years and we put a lot of weight on their recommendations." says Cass Bayley. "A referral from a bureau really helps us to narrow the field. We tell the bureau about our audience, what we're looking for and the budget we have to work with and they give us a short list. Then we dig further by looking at videos, getting references and testimonials. If it's a high-priced speaker, we always like to see him or her in person before hiring. Finally, we call other meeting planners to get advice and feedback."

"With a meeting planner's reputation on the line, they can't afford to take any risks," says Sarah Fitting of Bravo Management Group. "A bad presentation affects the entire conference. We at Bravo tend not to work directly with speakers. We prefer to work with bureaus. Having a good working relationship with a bureau helps to avoid any awkward situations. We rely on their expertise to help us match our clients' needs with the appropriate speakers. The bureaus are much more in touch with what their product is, who the latest speakers are and any new development in their speaker's repertoire."

Meeting planners have so many details to look after that leaving the bureau in charge of the latest development in the speaking world makes a lot of sense. At Bravo, Sarah Fitting talks to the bureau's agent about possible fits for an upcoming meeting, then does some brainstorming around the client and gives the bureau a sense of the client culture and the goal of the meeting. It's through this sorting process of elimination that just the right fit is found.

Speaker Marcia Wieder likes to be a part of this process from the start. Marcia ran a multi-million dollar marketing business in Washington, D.C. and then left it all behind to follow her dream of writing and speaking about following one's passion. "Since I'm a Dream Coach," she says, "I always like to have an intimate conversation with the meeting planner so that I can determine what their client's vision is for the meeting. There are the logistics, of course, but there's also the vision – and I need to know what that is."

Marcia is willing to do what it takes to find out. "When a meeting planner submits my name, I'm happy to talk to the client or have a three-way conversation. That gives me a strong sense of what the objectives are for the convention."

There's an added benefit for the meeting planner. "With my background in sales, I can often close the sale. I'm happy to do that. I consider myself not as a star, but as a member of the meeting planner's team."

That helps to avoid what Sarah Fitting calls one of the biggest nightmares for planners. "To have a speaker talk about something completely irrelevant to the client's goals makes everyone involved look really bad. A good bureau or agency will steer me away from making those kinds of mistakes. Speakers need to make sure they have adequate representation with a bureau, simply because it makes our lives so much easier. When a speaker is represented, we know that they're user-tested. An agent will tell us that this particular speaker may not be right for a young crowd. Bureaus offer great guidance."

On occasion, there's a need to educate the client. Sometimes a client will tell the meeting planner they want to hire a certain speaker. After talking to a bureau, the meeting planner may discover that that particular speaker is not right for the convention and the client has to be diplomatically persuaded to consider another speaker.

Relationships are based on trust. Any bureau who tries to flog a high priced speaker without considering whether that speaker is right for a particular conference will not stay in business long. It's when bureaus and meeting planners work in synergy towards the same ends that magic happens. The right speaker, after all, can make or break a conference.

Finding Clients

Your best leads for paid speaking engagements will come from your audience members. And your second best sources of leads will come from a company CEO who belongs to the same organization you do. The third best source of leads is the organizer of association, government or corporate conferences for your target audience. Other sources of leads are independent meeting planners and referrals from other speakers.

The truth is there are more leads out there than you would ever, in your lifetime, have time to follow up. If you're not getting all the bookings you want, the problem is not a lack of leads. The problem is a lack of vision to see the opportunities. That's something you can change.

When you're at a hotel or convention center check out the posted Calendar of Events to see what other meetings are taking place. When you're attending a meeting, collect everyone's business card and make a quick notation on the back stating where and when you met this person and anything that might be relevant. Then add all the pertinent names and addresses to your database.

When you're ready to make that call to the meeting planner or convention organizers, make sure you know exactly what you want to achieve from the call and have your telephone script ready. A good outcome is a request for your one-page faxable sheet. A great outcome is to set up a face-to-face meeting. A soft-sell approach always works best.

Feel free to deviate from the following script but use it as a foundation.

"Hello, my name is ... and I understand you're in charge of organizing the upcoming conference for the Teacher's Association this year. Have you decided on a theme for the conference? I have a speech I think would fit in very well with that theme. Do you have all your speakers lined up or may I send you an outline and bio? Do you prefer e-mail or regular mail?"

You also want to know what their budget is for a speaker for that event and who the decision-maker is. If the decision is made by a committee, then inquire when the committee will meet next and when they'll be making a final decision.

The world of paid professional speaking is still a buyer's market so a soft sell is the only appropriate approach to the buyer. And if you have a contact that can make your cold call a warm one, by all means, use it.

Cold calling can be an intimidating proposition but once that initial call has taken place, any further calls are warm. You may have to make as many as 10 cold calls to get a good lead and many more to get a solid booking. In the meantime, you're building up a relationship and you will get returns on that two years down the road. At the very least, you're increasing your name recognition and improving your sales and marketing skills.

Your ratio of solid leads to phone calls will improve as you gain confidence in your selling and marketing skills. The optimal time to call is between 9 and 10 in the morning from Monday to Friday.

Your enthusiasm and passion for what you're doing is contagious so before you pick up that phone, remind yourself of what your purpose is and convey that to the buyer.

Basically, your clients will come from associations, governments, non-profits or corporate markets, with the corporate markets being the highest paying. Here are some resources for finding these various markets in both Canada and the U. S.

Non-Profits
www.charityvillage.com
www.guidestar.org

Associations
Associations Canada
www.greyhouse.com

Encyclopedia of Foundations (U. S.)
www.greenwood.com

The Directory of National Trade and Professional Associations
www.columbiabooks.com

Yearbook of Experts and Authorities
www.expertclick.com

Sources Media Directory
www.sources.com

Government
Society of Government Meeting Professionals
www.sgmp.org

Women's Conferences
http://www.allconferences.net

Corporate Market
www.hoovers.com
www.sgmp.org

Create your own plan for approaching your prospective clients. Once you've defined your audience, find out what associations they belong to and begin to create an ongoing strategy for contacting them systematically and regularly. Don't leave anything to chance.

How will you make yourself visible to your clients?

Create a foolproof marketing plan for yourself and be accountable. Track your own progress or pair up with another speaker and be accountable to each other. Continue to tweak your marketing plan as you discover what tactics work best and
what tactics need to be left behind.

There's a gold mine of information in this chapter. Some will mine it, others won't.

Which group will you fall into?

CHAPTER 8

Leaving $$$ on the Table?
with Dr. Charles Petty, PhD, CSP, CPAE

"If you're lonely, get a dog. If you want to practice, get a volunteer audience. Only if you think you can improve an individual's and/or organization's well-being, however, should you try to get a client."

Alan Weiss

"**I** know I leave money on the table," says Charles Petty.

Dr. Petty has what he refers to as a mid-level topic and so far he's resisted his colleagues' advice to up his normal fee of $5,000 and to develop and push product sales.

Here is Dr. Petty's perspective in his own words:

"In order to learn from how I got here, it is important to look at where I am now. Within the National Speakers Association there are keynoters, consultants, trainers and entertainers. Each is unique and in each case, success is predicated upon different principles.

"My career is basically as a keynote speaker, consisting primarily of one night stands. A normal year I'll give presentations to 80 to 120 different clients. Fewer than 80 presentations is considered a bad year and more than 120 is very difficult to achieve from a schedule/travel standpoint. Geographically, I give speeches each year in 30 to 35 different states and two to four countries.

"Most speaking careers evolve. A good rule is that when your speaking is generating about 40% of what you are earning at a day job, then your chances of making it as a speaker are favorable. However, having a passion for speaking does not always mean you are a talented speaker. Neither passion nor belief in yourself can produce a successful speaking career. Granted that success does depend upon passion and belief in yourself but these can not stand alone. It takes much more. There are a lot of people trying to make it in this business who should be doing something else for a living.

"From 1977 to 1985 I was on the senior staff of the Governor of North Carolina. When governors go out of office, staff members are given that same opportunity. At that time I was presenting a number of family-life conferences in religious settings and would receive an honorarium. Presentations to the secular world were considered part of my government job and thus were free.

"Having received encouragement from several speakers that I could make it, it felt right to become a professional speaker. My wife was a homemaker and we had two teenage sons. Produce quickly or perish were my options.

"Because business and trade associations were accustomed to my speaking for free, they were reluctant to pay. Quickly every speaker learns what he or she has in common with a prostitute: neither one can afford to give it away for very long and stay in business.

"Had the second year duplicated the first, my career would have lasted one year. Luckily, my income increased 87% the second year and has increased almost every year for the past 20 years.

"I am a contrarian, as my mode of operation is different from most successful speakers. I have done very little cold-calling or mailing. If one plays the numbers and scatters tons of materials to the wind, chances are some one will hire you. But for every yes, there are a hundred no's. Very few speakers can take that volume of rejection. One resistant audience member can consume many speakers and if 99% of the audience were negative, it would be more than most egos could withstand, certainly mine.

"To counter the rejection, new speakers often hire a staff member to market. The problem is that beginning speakers have little income and need to minimize expenses. The second problem is that no one knows the speaker as well as the speaker. For example, I was reared on a farm. Very few of the bureau sales people who market me know that and consequently might fail to set the hook with an agriculture group. Often all it takes to make the deal is one sentence. One insight.

"Not having a full-time staff person has saved my career in the beginning and has cost me money the past few years. The person who works with me is part-time and basically covers the client's request for information, manages the calendar and refuses to make the coffee. She clearly stated she would not cold-market and doesn't. Honestly, she is often bored with nothing to do. But all she has to do is save a few engagements, cover a few emergencies, and she earns her salary.

"My marketing strategy is there, it is just a bit different from most. Here is what has worked for me and is what I call warm-marketing.

"Have something to say that other people want to hear. My basic presentation is 'Climbing The Ladder Of Success And Taking Your Family With You.' Not everyone wants to hear that topic but enough do to keep me busy. Obviously, I speak on several other topics but family is what I am known for. The advantage of 'family' is that it cuts across all industries and trade associations. My branding is a topic not an industry. Because of 9/11, family has become more important on the speaking chart although it will never be a big-buck topic.

"Whatever you say, say it well. The best advertising is when a speaker hits a home run. Many audiences have potential spin-off customers sitting there. Those are the best leads you will ever have.

"After a presentation if no one ever comes up and says, 'We want you to come speak to our group,' then either your topic is too limited or your delivery is sub-par. I spoke to a state banking association and the executive director asked if he could recommend me to his 49 counterparts. Not only did I consent, but also offered to send each of them my press kit. At least 15 state associations booked me because of his recommendation and that has resulted in my speaking to a number of individual banks. Incidentally, I do not follow up on kits mailed. If after looking at my material, the program planner does not even care enough to call, why should I bother? I like to speak not beg.

"Have something to say that others will pay a reasonable fee to hear. The downside to family is that it falls into the mid to low fee range. I know my fee will never reach the bragging-in-the-hallway stage. But if one does enough volume, it is a good living. Many speakers overcharge for what their topic or skill will bear. When you move up the fee scale you are in competition with all the other speakers and topics at that level. Plus fewer groups have that fee so the competition is stiffer and the clients fewer. My strategy is to stay affordable.

"Write an introduction and ask the client to use it. In that introduction indicate the groups you speak to: i.e. businesses, trade associations, educators, etc. Amazingly, many audience members assume you just speak to the type of group you are addressing. Help audiences realize that your remarks will fit many groups and situations.

"Always remember that your primary responsibility as a speaker is not to the audience. It is to the program planner. The one who is held responsible for your being there is the one you take care of first. Never criticize, no matter how strong the temptation. These are the people who can invite you back and recommend you to their network, which can easily become a major source of business. In fact, within 24 hours of returning home from an engagement I put a thank-you letter in the mail. I stood behind a speaker who had preceded me on the program and he was blasting the program planner. In exasperation she said, "Well, we did the best we could." His reply was, "Your best wasn't good enough. You will have to do better next time." Next time? There will not be a next time for him.

"Never offend the audience. Challenge, probe, push, stretch, even irritate but don't offend. Some humor, ethnic remarks, sexist comments, four-letter words are the kiss of death. Sure a few in the audience like down and dirty but they rarely are the ones who hire or recommend a speaker. Give them a reason to hire you not one not to hire you.

"Be easy to work with. There is a strange paradox in our business. The higher the fee, the more demanding a speaker becomes. Celebrity speakers are in another world and few of us are celebrities. However, all of us should go to bed at night thanking God for the abilities and opportunity to do what we do. Making more money in 30 minutes than most people do in one or two months is great incentive to be humble. There are speakers who demand new 100% cotton sheets on their hotel bed. Others insist on a certain brand of water on the podium and it must be at an exact temperature. Program planners have what every speaker needs: an audience and money. If these planners ever wake up and discover that they have all the power in this business, prima donnas are doomed. From thousands of speakers to choose from, why pick a jerk? My presentations work best under certain circumstances but if those circumstances change, then so do I, with a smile. Recently on a program I was introduced six minutes before the trap door was to open. I spoke six minutes and sat down.

"Keep your PR material updated. The shelf life of much material is quite limited. Websites must be updated quarterly. Videos redone every two or three years. Photographs should be no more than one or two years old and avoid glamour shots. You do not want the meeting planner to do a double take when seeing you for the first time. I had a digital photo done recently and the photographer asked, "Shall I remove that blemish? Make you teeth whiter? Eyes whiter?" I declined because I want to look better than my photo. "Bait and switch" alienates program planners. Don't spend too much money on hard copy when much of it can be downloaded from your website. Print what you can, as tossing 10,000 dated brochures reflects badly on your marketing plan! When I bought a computer the sales person said, "This model will suffice for a couple of years." I'm thinking, "Make that for a lifetime." If used as a glorified typewriter, it should last a long time. Resist spending too much on equipment or showy things that do not pay for themselves. Marketing is expensive when done right and costly when done wrong.

"Sell products judiciously. I leave a lot of money on the table and lose future speaking engagements by not aggressively selling products. I will sell back-of-the- room tapes and CDs, but this is very low key (two sentences toward the end of my presentation) and is done on the honor system. Throw $20 in the bag and get a set of tapes. This approach is contrary to what most speakers promote and I accept their rationale. But for me I want to be a speaker not a bookstore on wheels. Plus, I want to be invited back. At a recent event speakers were asked not to sell products at the back of the room. No problem for me. Another speaker insisted on two long tables to display all of his products and constantly mentioned them in his presentation. I said to the meeting planner, 'I thought we were not to sell products at this convention.' 'You weren't,' she replied, 'but he showed up with his products, insisted on tables, and I am furious.' Do you think he will ever be invited back by that planner? Or recommended to others? I have to sell a lot of product to equal a full fee and usually will err on the side of walking softly. Sure I lose a lot of money by not being aggressive but I make a lot of money, sleep well, write no letters of apology and have no pangs of guilt.

"Don't market at every opportunity. One of my best speaker friends markets wherever he goes. When we eat in a restaurant he constantly is 'on', entertaining everyone whether they want to be or not. At NSA some presenters advise you to fly first class and let everyone there know you are looking for business. I fly frequently and usually get bumped up to first class. Regardless of whom I am sitting beside, I do not hustle him or her. If my seat mate tried to sell me insurance, I would be irritated. If my seat mate begs to know what I do, then he will get a low pressure sales pitch.

"Be professional. Nothing sells quite like professionalism. This concept must permeate everything you do. How you dress, both on and off the platform, says volumes about you. Your materials must look first class. Misspellings are the kiss of death. Failing to return telephone calls, e-mails and letters promptly means another speaker will take your business. Work in a sweat suit from your home office, but sound dressed up. Show up long before you are to speak. Quit on time even if someone prior to you has stolen some of your time. When you arrive at the hotel, inform the meeting planner that you are there, alive and well, ready to go the next morning. If a bureau has booked you, call upon arrival and assure them no backup will be needed – unless you die in the night! Take care of business professionally or someone else will take your business.

"Working with bureaus is smart for both the client and speaker. Clients should book through bureaus for it gives them a true account of the speaker and serves as a buffer when things go badly. Speakers should realize that bureaus are partners with them and both should profit from the efforts of the other. New speakers must realize that few bureaus will take a chance on an inexperienced speaker. If a speaker fouls up, he will usually get paid anyway but the bureau will have lost a client forever.

"The average bureau has between 6,000 and 10,000 speakers in its data bank. If the client wants three recommendations, the bureau will send out the names of experienced thoroughbreds. Winners every time. Working with bureaus means I have a bureau-friendly website and PR materials. It also means that all spin offs go back through the bureau. Win-win is the goal when working with bureaus. I am realistic in knowing that bureaus do not have my best interests at heart. If a client hesitates in hiring me for any reason, the bureau will promote another speaker in a heart beat. When there is a good fit and trust level between a speaker and bureau, both can profit, as I do with several bureaus.

"My approach to marketing does not focus on making it happen. It is a passive approach and income can vary from year to year. However, it has worked for me for twenty years. I hit six-figures the third year of speaking full-time and have never looked back. Learning to know what is really important is critical to discovering happiness. Having a lot of money does bring security and the ability to be generous with other and valued causes."

"But how much is enough? When does it ever stop? When will there ever be time for family, faith, friends and yourself? It is important to remember that your life and career hang from a very thin thread. One serious illnesses or accident – all it takes is one – and your career, if not over, can be greatly impeded. So, do what is really important in life and let a few gigs go to someone else – preferably to me!

"Speaking is a wonderful, blest career. Enjoy the ride and when it is over, get off graciously."

Dr. Petty can be reached at www.charlespetty.com.

CHAPTER 9

Get the Whole Town Talking
PR that Rocks

"We don't see things as they are. We see things as we are."
Anais Nin

Press campaigns need to be part of your marketing mix. While they're not income-generating in a direct way, they're an essential part of building a foundation. Schedule them every four to six months. Find a press-worthy angle for your new positioning statement or for one of your new keynote addresses. Be creative. I created a Talent Search as a vehicle for a re-launch of my bureau. What can you do to grab attention in an overly stimulated world?

Armed with an up-to-date media directory, write up a compelling press release. Ian Taylor, author of Never Say No Comment, compares sending out press releases to going fishing. "You have to know what the fish are looking for, how to bait them and how to land them on any given news day. If your news releases are failing, you probably haven't written them to read and sound like a news story. Chances are your present news releases sound like a PR promotion piece or paid advertising posing as news. Or else they're so bureaucratic that the reader can't easily understand what you're saying without having to translate the copy into plain talk."

Taylor recommends writing your news release in Media Speak. That simply means that your writing style matches the news style. "Your core news release message must be positioned in the public interest; it must be written in plain talk; and it must reflect your organization's professionalism so that little editing is required by newsrooms in order to create a final news story."

Here are Taylor's tips for making your news release stand out in a crowd.

- Read your news release out loud, like a radio reporter would.
- Rewrite it until you make it sound like a real news story.
- Always write in the third person.
- Target a Grade 8 or lower comprehension level.
- Keep the writing tight, fact-filled and interesting.
- Write short sentences and keep your paragraphs short, just like newspapers do. This results in more white space on the page and draws the reader into the words, not away from them.
- Notice how newspaper articles look on the page. See how short the paragraphs are.
- Count the words or check the time of news stories. If the typical TV news item is 90 seconds, that's about 200 words. If your goal is to create a 90-second news story, write a 200-word news release and no more.
- Add extra material as detailed "backgrounders."

For more detailed information from Ian on your press release, visit his website: .www.neversaynocomment.com.

Fax that press release to anywhere from 50 to 500 media outlets. Pick out 25 of the top prospects in your list and call them to follow up. Follow-up here is a crucial step.

If your audience is in the U.S., call National Trade and Professional Associations of the U. S. at 202-898-0662 or The Directory of Memberships and News Sources (National Press Club) at 202-662-7500. In Canada, visit http://www.sources.com to request a Canadian media directory.

What, exactly, do you want in return for your appearance or press coverage? If the answer is more clients as well as name recognition, make sure you make a pitch along with your contact information and also ensure what you have to offer is crystal clear. This needs to be done very naturally or you'll turn reporters off. They're not paid to promote you.

You'll need to modify your media approach if your long-term plan is to have a regular television show or a syndicated column in a local newspaper.

Media exposure in most cases reaches individuals rather than corporations, but each of those individuals has a network and most work for corporations so it's a worthwhile venture.

Make good quality copies of any press you get. These will be part of your promotional kit.

Go forth with a trumpet or a bugle rather than a flute. Get out into the world in a large way and announce yourself boldly. Be highly enthusiastic about who you are, and what you have to offer in the marketplace. Share that enthusiasm with everyone you meet.

Along with your media campaign, start networking in a very strategic way and plan to make yourself a household word so that the media comes to you.

Target one or two niche markets that your prospective clients belong to and join their associations. If you're targeting the travel market, then check out the Tourism and Convention Bureau in your area, the Hotel Sales and Marketing Association and the National Hotel Association. Also look into SITE (Society of Incentive and Travel Executives), and subscribe (as well as contribute) to Meeting and Incentive Travel Magazine and Corporate Travel Magazine. Become totally familiar with and well-networked in your particular niche market. If your niche is in the engineering field, then research that area and find the appropriate journals, conventions and associations you need to be part of.

Begin to submit articles to the publications and newsletters in your target market area. Add a blurb to the end of each article, letting readers know who you are, what you have to offer and how you can be contacted.

Getting good press boosts your Google count, your profile, your client base and your business.

When was the last time you appeared on radio or television? Is it time to plan next year's press campaign? The results are worth it.

Here's a sample press release from the website, www.marketingsource.com

FOR IMMEDIATE RELEASE:

CONTACT:
Contact Person
Company Name
Voice Phone Number
FAX Number
Email Address
Website URL
XYZ, Inc. Announces Widget to Maximize Customer Response Rate

This headline is one of the most important components of the press release as this needs to "grab the attention" of the editor. It should be in bold type and a font that is larger than the body text. Preferred type fonts are Arial, Times New Roman, or Verdana. Keep the headline to 80-125 characters maximum. Capitalize every word with the exception of "a", "the" "an" or any word that is three characters or less.

<City>, <State>, <Date> – Your first paragraph of the release should be written in a clear and concise manner. The opening sentence contains the most important information; keep it to 25 words or less. Never take for granted that the reader has read your headline. It needs contain information that will "entice" the reader. Remember, your story

must be newsworthy and factual; don't make it a sales pitch or it will end up in the trash.

Answer the questions "who", "what", "when", "where", "why" and "how". Your text should include pertinent information about your product, service or event. If writing about a product, make sure to include details on when the product is available, where it can be purchased and the cost. If you're writing about an event, include the date, location of the event and any other pertinent information. You should include a quote from someone that is a credible source of information; include their title or position with the company, and why they are considered a credible source. Always include information on any awards they have won, articles they've published or interviews they have given.

Keep your sentences and paragraphs short; a paragraph should be no more than 3-4 sentences. Your release should be between 500 to 800 words, written in a word processing program, and spell checked for errors. Don't forget to proofread for grammatical errors. The mood of the release should be factual, not hyped; don't use a sales pitch as it will ruin your credibility with the reader.

The last paragraph before the company information should read: For additional information on (put in the subject of this release), contact "name" or visit www.yoururl.com. If you offer a sample, copy or demo, put the information in here. You can also include details on product availability, trademark acknowledgment, etc. in this area of the release.

ABOUT <COMPANY> - Include a brief description of your company along with the products and services it provides.

- END -

At the end of the release, you need to indicate that the release is ended. This lets the journalists know they have received the entire release. Type "End" on the first line after your text is completed. If your release goes over one page, type "MORE" at the bottom of the first page.

CHAPTER 10

Who Needs the Bureaus?
Actually You Do - Here's Why

*"What others say about you and your product, service or
business is at least 1,000 times more convincing than what you
say, even if you are 1,000 times more eloquent."*

Dan Kennedy

It's often said that it's harder to get a literary agent than a
publisher. So, several years ago, when a literary agent called me, saying
she loved my writing, that it just jumped off the page and she wanted to
represent me, I knew that Fame and Fortune were sure to follow. Clearly, I
was on the Fast Track! Finally.

Well, not quite.

My little fantasy was nice while it lasted but the truth is this – it
really, REALLY doesn't work like that.

Are you listening? This may apply to you.

Have you felt that way with bureaus? When bureaus agree to add
you to their roster, do visions of multiple bookings and living happily ever
after dance in your head?

Well, back to my agent. She wasn't based in Toronto, didn't use e-
mail (!!) and couldn't get a publisher for my book. After two years, we
agreed to part ways.

There's a lesson here.

With very few exceptions, an agent, whether in the speaking or
publishing field, is not going to make or break you. Only you can do that.
Fame and fortune never depend on outside sources but on your own
efforts. And that's a universal law I'm sure!

If you're not already extremely successful, an agent will usually not
be very helpful.

Same with bureaus.

I've heard it said that bureaus are only interested in you when you don't need them. There is a grain of truth here but let's reframe this. Bureaus can only market you when you've successfully marketed yourself.

I've also heard that bureaus are rip-off artists, taking a huge commission simply for sending off a contract. Not even a grain of truth in that in my experience.

Well, maybe a small grain. There are a handful of shady people in any profession. The problem is that many professional speakers – upbeat, optimistic and eager to follow their dream – are particularly vulnerable to them. You need to be discerning.

In his book Speaking for Millions: How to Make Really Big Money as a Professional Speaker, here's what author Fred Gleeck has to say about bureaus:

"Here's the major dilemma for a speaker. When you need the bureaus, they don't need you. After you have established yourself as a speaker, they will get calls for you and all they will do is call you up and get a huge chunk of your fee for just making a phone call or two. This, to me, is a royal rip-off.

"Talk to the bureaus and they will give you a big song and dance about how much work they have to do and how much overhead they have. Baloney! For the most part, they are vastly overpaid in the majority of situations."

While I can understand Gleeck's perspective, I think it's both short-sighted and outdated. He's looking at things from a personal perspective rather than a business perspective.

The broader picture is that bureaus have done a lot for the speaking profession in general.

The real truth is that speaker's bureaus have raised the profile of the entire profession of speaking, just as unions have raised the profile of unacceptable working conditions even in non-unionized shops.

So if you're earning a healthy income as a professional speaker, thank all the speaker's bureaus out there for their part in educating clients on the need to pay well for a top speaker.

Bureaus have really elevated the entire speaking profession and you, as a speaker, benefit from that in terms of being able to ask for higher fees and also just getting greater visibility.

The speaking profession is an expensive field to market in and bureaus certainly do have a much higher overhead than the individual speaker. Bureaus have offices and staff to maintain, websites to update, directories to print and high phone and postal charges.

Being represented by bureaus is not going to rescue your speaking career. However, being listed with reputable bureaus will add an income stream, as well as enhance your credibility and raise your profile.

Bureaus who carry certain speakers exclusively have been known to push their exclusive speakers to their clients at the cost of the other speakers they carry. Ethical bureaus won't do that, though.

It's rarely in a speaker's best interest to go exclusively with any bureau.

As for ways to increase your chances to be represented by the top bureaus, take a tip from some speakers who go the extra mile when they work with bureaus.

Kare Anderson, for example, considers the bureau a client as well as the group she speaks to and she spends time nurturing the relationship. Kare's policy is this: whenever a bureau books her for an engagement, she gives the bureau a lead on another engagement. That places her front and centre in the bureau's mind when recommending speakers for their clients.

Smart move.

CSP Jim Cathcart's approach to bureaus was to declare 1992 The Year of the Bureau. Here's what he says:

"In 1992, before the Web and Internet, I told my staff it was the year of the bureau. We were to think like a bureau. What kind of information did bureaus need and how could they quickly access it?

"We made sure everything we produced was bureau-friendly and I created a handbook on how to sell Jim Cathcart. It cost $25 to create it. I spent thousands of dollars sending it out to bureaus and agents.

"Really, it was a website in print form. We had my policies on travel and other expenses, speech content, products, client list, testimonials, etc. It was difficult maintaining updates.

"I also created an article, 10 Vital Issues for Bureaus. I sent one at a time to bureaus and then sent the booklet out to agents. Eventually, I trashed the booklet and put it on my website. It was fully functioning virtually overnight."

Jim's approach makes bureaus very eager to book him.

Keeping in touch with bureaus as to new developments in your career, or just to say hello from time to time, is a great way to keep yourself front and center in their awareness.

Who Needs the Bureaus?

You do, actually. Unless you're one of those very rare speakers – about one or two percent – whose business comes solely from word of mouth, you need bureaus.

Here's why. Clients tend to book speakers through bureaus because they know that they can count on the bureau's expertise and reputation to make recommendations on hiring the right speaker for the job.

I believe the trend to book through bureaus rather than go directly to the speaker will increase. The reason is obvious. A bureau can give an unbiased recommendation. I've had clients ask about speakers who clearly aren't a good match for their event. So I've had to gently steer them to another speaker who is, in my view, a better fit and tell them why I feel that way.

Here's the thing. You, as a speaker, can call ABC Association and say, "I hear you've got a conference coming up and are looking for a speaker – I'd be perfect for the job." Well, sure you would be – if you say so....

Still, the person on the other end of the phone might wonder if you're really being objective about your abilities or if you just want the speaking engagement and the fat fee that goes with it.

On the other hand, when a bureau says, "Given your needs and budget, I'd recommend either Charley, Susan or Sam for this engagement," the buyer pays attention.

Bureaus simply can't try to fit a speaker into the wrong slot or they'd go right out of business. They have to make a recommendation based on which of their speakers they think is right for this particular booking and this audience.

And contained in the previous paragraph is the first clue on how to work well with bureaus.

As you're listing with a bureau, let them know whether you specialize in keynotes or training and paint a profile of your ideal client. What groups are you most comfortable with?

Don't overstate your case. Don't slip into hyperbole. Don't paint a false picture. It will come back to bite you later when you're in front of a group that's not right for you.

Getting Listed

When are you ready to be listed with a bureau? Generally speaking, you're ready to approach the bureaus when you're in the $5,000 fee range, have great materials, a video, a good client list and solid testimonials.

On top of all this, you'll also need some way of standing out from the crowd. If you speak about customer service, how are you different from others? You need to be able to name your point of differentiation.

And you need to have a great track record of marketing yourself.

I, and I'm sure other bureaus, have had speakers say, "I love to do the speaking but I hate to market." They've achieved a certain expertise in their particular area and now want to have a bigger impact in the marketplace.

But, I suspect, it's lack of confidence that keeps them stuck when it comes to marketing themselves.

And here's the most important sentence in this entire book:

If you don't believe in yourself and what you have to offer enough to go out and start telling the world about it, how can I possibly be successful marketing you?

Doesn't it occur to you that you're beginning by marketing to me and unless you convey an amazing belief in yourself, the marketing will fall flat?

And you've just rendered me unable to market you to anyone else.

When your positioning is great and your message powerful, you'll be so pumped about it, you'll market with every breath you take.

Ask Derrick Sweet, for example. Derrick's one of the most enthusiastic and upbeat people I've ever met. Derrick puts his all into everything he does and he knows he's good. So do his clients. So do bureaus. His enthusiasm makes it easy to market him.

If you work with a bureau, your materials need to be bureau-friendly. Your one-pager needs to have the bureau's contact information on it rather than yours. Creating a bureau-friendly mirror-image website is a great way to increase your bookings with bureaus. It's an exact copy of your website without the contact information.

For an excellent example of a great bureau-friendly website go to: http://www.pete-luckett.com.

Today's Hot Topics

When speakers come to me asking me what the hot topics are, I tell them they're asking the wrong question.

I then ask what it is they're passionate about, what would they speak about even if they're weren't being paid. What motivated them to enter this profession in the first place?

We then take that topic or concept and adapt it to fit into the marketplace. So please don't ask what the hot topics are and then twist yourself like a pretzel to fit into something that's not a good match for you.

It just doesn't work and your bookings (or lack thereof) will reflect that.

Instead, take your passion and brilliance and find the hook into the marketplace.

At Speakers Gold, we find that what buyers are looking for is a combination of motivation, entertainment and solid information. In other words, they want it all. Adventure speakers are very popular, as long as they customize their speech for the audience and leave behind a practical message that's relevant to the group.

According to independent meeting planner Cass Bayley, "Motivation is not hot right now. People want hard core specifics they can put into practice. Humorous speakers who can inform and entertain an audience are always popular. Health and lifestyle is in demand, as are balance, stress, change management and ethics."

Global leadership and competing in global markets are very popular topics right now.

Meeting News recently asked meeting planners which type of

keynote speaker was the most appealing to their groups these days. 44% said someone famous for overcoming obstacles or achieving great things. Another 34% preferred an expert or researcher in their industry. On the bottom of the list were industry execs and politicians/authors "of good repute." The bottom line is two-fold here: 1) the market is pretty split between the feel-good types and substantial information in the speech creating enough opportunities for both kinds of speakers and 2) being an author, even with a popular book, isn't enough.

Why not combine motivation with great information? First tell me why I should care about the information you're about to relay. Otherwise, you might as well just hand me a book to read. Then give me great new information or old information that's been reconfigured. It doesn't get any better than that!

Rather than dance to the tune of an ever-evolving marketplace, it's better to find your own financially viable niche, then continue to develop and expand upon it. Instead of staking your financial future on booking one keynote at a time, drill down into your area of expertise and begin to provide Think Tanks, Boot Camps, Intensive Weekends or long-term consulting for your clients. You want to offer an entire menu of services so that you're flexible.

Logistics, Fees and Commissions

Bureau commissions, it seems, have a wide spread, ranging from 35% to 25% commission. Most bureaus charge 30% and some charge 25%. Some charge for a listing on the website, others offer "packages" and still others will charge you to be in a brochure, in the annual showcase or on the website. Ask before you list.

It doesn't hurt to test, although personally when I was starting out as a speaker, I paid to be included in a mail-out with one bureau and for a listing in a brochure with another bureau and got absolutely no returns. Proceed with caution when you're spending money on advertising.

Here's how it works with most bureaus. They get an inquiry from a client and feel that you're a suitable match. They e-mail the client your one-pager along with the promotional material of a couple of other speakers so the client has a choice. Or they direct the client to your page on their website and may also suggest that the client check another speaker or two. The bureau then follows up with a phone call.

Until the contract has been signed or the speaker even decided upon, the bureau may ask two or three speakers in the running to hold the date as a courtesy and most speakers are willing to do this.

If you've been asked to hold a date until a decision has been made, two or three days seems a fair amount of time to hold the date. If you get a solid offer for the same day and time, then alert the bureau that the client needs to make a decision right away or risk losing you.

Bureaus always should advise you to release that date if the booking goes to someone else or falls through. In practice, though, many bureaus don't follow up and you're left dangling. After a few days, call the bureau and inquire as to whether you should release that date or continue to hold it. If you don't hear back, assume the booking fell through.

When the client's seriously interested in hiring you, some bureaus will put you directly in touch with the client to discuss the event, some bureaus won't until the contract's been signed. Because we at Speakers Gold deliberately have a small select roster, we don't hesitate to put our speakers directly in touch with the client to close the deal when necessary. Reputable bureaus will have you contact the client before the event so you can customize your speech.

What does it mean to customize the speech? Add the company logo to your materials and work their name into your speech? No! Customize means an intensive interview or preliminary questionnaire with the buyer, the meeting planner and a couple of people who will be in the audience to make sure that your speech fulfills the buyer's objectives. Read Orvel Ray Wilson's chapter in this book to get an idea of the lengths he goes to in order to customize his speech or training.

Once the booking's confirmed verbally and the date fixed, the bureau faxes or e-mails a contract to the client. At this stage, the bureau requires a 50% deposit to hold the date.

A verbal agreement is not always worth very much in this field. You only consider the booking solid once that 50% deposit has been received by the bureau.

Most bureaus take their commission out of that initial deposit and mail the balance to the speaker. Some bureaus hold that entire 50% deposit in case of a cancellation. In case the client cancels? No. In case the speaker doesn't show up. However, as Alan Weiss points out, the speaker has absolutely no protection if the bureau goes out of business before the speaker gets paid. In my opinion, the best practice of a bureau is to take the commission out of the deposit check and pass the remainder directly on to the speaker.

Some bureaus have been known to be very slow in mailing out that initial check, and there have been horror stories of a few bureaus that have gone out of business while still owing the speaker money.

They are the exception, though.

When working with a bureau, ask them what their policy is on payment.

The bureau should request that the final check be made out to and given to you on the day of the speaking engagement.

Expenses are billed afterward by the bureau and that check goes directly to you, unless you have what many bureaus recommend and that is a flat fee to cover your expenses. In that case, the bureau includes that in the initial contract.   No matter how you charge for expenses, bureaus take no commission on travel expenses.

They will often take a commission on book and product sales. And many bureaus will want a full commission on any follow-up business generated by the original speaking engagement.

In other words, if you speak to a group of XY Bank employees and you get booked to speak to all their other branches, most bureaus will take 25% of your fee for those subsequent engagements.

Again, you need to ask the bureau what their policy is.

Some bureaus have an annual showcase where they feature their top speakers and invite meeting planners. Bookings are often confirmed at the event itself.

While these used to be held at the bureau's expense, they are now becoming profit centers for many bureaus who get sponsors for the event and also charge the speakers for being part of the showcase.

If you're asked to participate in a showcase for a fee, ask how many bookings they expect as a result. Then talk to other speakers who have been in previous showcases to see what the results were. Make your own decision based on your findings.

Encore

How do you get repeat bookings from a bureau?

Derrick Sweet, I think, mastered that technique right off the bat.

He started off offering Speakers Gold a huge commission for initial bookings.

"It's fine with me," he said.   "I just want to get out there and speak."

And whenever he was booked, Derrick came back with leads from the engagement that he passed on directly to the bureau. This is a great way of making friends for life with bureaus.

Most of the speakers I represent are great. I can't name you in person though I would love to. You know who you are. You are completely honest and accommodating and if I ask you to meet with the client before the event, you're happy to do so. You always call me afterwards to say how it went and what possibilities there are for the future. You are real partners and a joy to work with. Thank you. You are the reason I'm in this business.

Working With the Best

You enhance your reputation by working only with the best bureaus. When I spoke to Les Brown's agent, she said "Some bureaus just like to put Les on their roster but they never get him bookings." The bureaus list this easily recognizable big name more to enhance their reputation than to get him bookings.

So having a great roster with big names is no way to ensure that that particular bureau is actually the best. It just looks good online.

Ask around. Check with colleagues and friends. Ask how the bureau is to work with.

Find out what the bureau's policies are. Many bureaus consider the booking client to be their client and the speaker to be, well, kind of like an employee on contract.

Speakers Gold, along with Kim George of LimeLight Communications Group Inc. consider that both speakers and booking agents are our clients. That's the attitude you want to look for when considering a bureau to list with.

See what comes up when you google speakers bureaus. Check out the top 10 bureaus' websites to see how credible they appear. Who else do they carry? How professional is their website?

Going Exclusive

Should you go exclusive with one bureau? Well, that's not an easy question to answer. So the answer is basically "sometimes."

It all depends on how many speaking gigs you want. If a bureau can supply that number (along with those engagements you get yourself), then it might make sense to go exclusive.

I have an exclusive arrangement with a few of the speakers I represent. In exchange for the exclusivity arrangement, I actively promote these speakers by either having them appear in my annual showcase or by placing their articles in periodicals, enhancing their material, consulting with them and so on. I do what I can to make sure the arrangement is in the speaker's best interest as well as mine.

When a bureau builds up its reputation to the point of having a lot of repeat customers, the bureau can then offer an exclusive to their top speakers. The advantage to the bureau is that it keeps those much-in-demand speakers out of circulation. The only way other bureaus can book that speaker is to request a commission split with the bureau, which actually doesn't happen all that often.

If, for any reason, the bureau says no to splitting the commission with other bureaus then they're not honestly representing your best needs as a speaker.

Answering these critical questions will ensure that you will create a relationship with bureaus strategically, rather than by default.

- How will bureaus be part of your marketing mix?
- Which ones would you like to list with?

- How will you partner with them?
- What will make a bureau eager to work with you?
- How many bureau bookings would you like to have each month?

You need to consider what benefits a bureau would bring you as well as what value you and your speech bring to their table.

In almost every instance, it just makes good sense to have a bureau or two marketing on your behalf.

CHAPTER 11

Make Yourself Bureau-Friendly
with David Pace

"If a bureau isn't providing value, why should you pay them 25% of your income? If you continue to do this, it's not the bureau's fault. You are not managing that relationship."

Alan Weiss

David Pace is the owner of the Business Speakers Bureau. His bureau accepts speakers at a starting fee level of $3,500. Any speakers looking for representation from Pace's bureau also need a one-sheet marketing piece that is well-thought-out, well-designed and bureau-friendly along with great references, short topic outlines and a good photo.

Then there's the video!

"We in the U.S. seem to need a huge amount of video footage," David says. "Clients these days insist on seeing the speaker live, even those at the lower end of the scale. Every speaker – no exception – needs a DVD, CD or VCR that we can send out to our clients."

Business Speakers Bureau uses the services of Espeaker (http://www.espeaker.com) to access the speaker's streaming video - it's all on Espeaker's bureau-friendly website. This makes it much easier for their clients to get information quickly so they encourage their speakers to get listed with Espeaker. The speaker has control of the entire web content. They can change it at any time and it will be instantly put up. Speakers pay a maintenance fee and bureaus pay a subscription fee but it's not expensive.

David finds that many of his clients don't know what they want and rely on the bureau's expertise and advice. "Especially in the association market," he says. "Inexperienced meeting planners know they need something different, so they say send me what you have and then I have to dig to find out what they really need."

He finds that his time-strapped clients won't even open the proposal if he sends it out as an attachment, even when they've asked for it, so BSB also sends out hard copies. "We end up doing both," David says, "paper and online proposals. We'd lose business if we didn't do both."

In terms of commissions, Business Speakers Bureau charges 25%. "Bureaus often reduce their commission to 20% if the speaker's fee is more than $20,000. It's really important that speakers don't add on to their fee to compensate for the commission when booked through a bureau. If the speaker says 'My fee is $7,000,' we expect him to stick to that whether he's booked through us or directly. We spend horrendous amounts of time and energy to generate business for speakers. If we only get a 10% commission, it won't work. We have to make our money somehow."

As for the future, David believes that current trends will continue. "There's a flood of speakers and the market is sometimes saturated. When I see speakers raising their fees exponentially instead of modestly, it hurts their business because of the competitiveness of the market. A couple of our speakers have raised their fees twice in the last six months - one doubled the fee. They didn't consult with me about this and we're bound by what they decide. After September 11th, everyone held their fee for four or five years and now fees are skyrocketing. Speakers are not going to compensate for the money they lost in a tough market by hugely raising their fees suddenly. That will bite them."

Two of David's speakers represent the ideal in the industry. One of their top speakers – Michael Wicket – is a motivational sales trainer. "He's extremely thorough with the client," says David, "customizes his programs extensively through a lot of consultations with the client and is very good on the platform. He not only knows how to energize the group, but attendees walk away with solid information. The other speaker who jumps to mind is Walter Bond – a basketball athlete. He knows the client's interests and needs inside-out and uses customized examples with their jargon embedded in his speech. He recently did a program for a dental group and all of his examples related to dentistry. This always goes over well – we get 110% great feedback and referrals from every speech he gives."

David's advice to speakers is to create great materials, go the second mile for your clients and make sure you're in the right fee range for what the market will bear. And it goes without saying – choose the right bureaus to align yourself with!

David can be reached at www.bsbspeakers.com

CHAPTER 12

Winning the Numbers Game:
Gaining Clients by Putting the Odds in Your Favor

"We are what we repeatedly do. Excellence then is not an action but a habit."

Aristotle 384-322 B.C.

When professional speaker and business owner Derrick Sweet and I were talking about the speaking business, he said, "Cathleen, it's all a numbers game."

Derrick had a background in the financial industry so he knew what he was talking about. He knew that success was a simple equation that just needed to be figured out.

Derrick was 100% right.

Here are the questions you need to answer before creating your own equation:

- How many gigs do you want?
- Who are your clients?
- Where will you find your clients? (Look for an umbrella group).
- How many people do you need to phone or events do you need to attend to get a gig?
- How much time can you set aside for phone calls and meetings?
- How large (and current) is your database?
- How can you build that up?
- How will you use it to its best advantage?

Armed with a determination to discover the answers to these questions, Derrick forged ahead and began making phone calls, starting with contacts he'd made in the financial planning world.

Starting out, he offered to speak free of charge. He was as enthusiastic and energetic about those unpaid engagements as he later was about full-paying gigs.

After Derrick had accumulated some wonderful feedback from his non-paying clients, he began to charge a decent fee and stuck to it. (In the beginning, he was on a learning curve and he didn't turn anything down.) He hired David who was required to make 25 phone calls a day. While the fully paid speaking gigs still took some time to build up, the 25 phone calls a day really put Derrick's speaking career in motion.

That's where many speakers get stuck. That's the hardest part – to build up a momentum. Once you've done that, it's fairly easy to keep things in motion.

Derrick used a database management system to keep track of every lead and note the results of every phone call. Without that system, he simply wouldn't have been successful.

David started out on a salary and commission and within a few months went directly to a very hefty commission. Derrick and David were both happy.

Now before you run out and find someone to make 25 calls on your behalf, keep this in mind. David was successful in part because Derrick is such a powerhouse of enthusiasm and energy. Derrick was a constant power surge that kept David motivated and going even when he had a day full of voice mails or rejection.

Not many beginning speakers can hire full-time staff in the first year of business. It's a great way to move ahead quickly once you have mastered the marketing basics yourself.

It really is a numbers game. Derrick's on to something. It's also a matter of keeping good track of those numbers.

Create your own equation now. X number of phones calls times X number of follow-ups = X number of gigs. Now calculate the time and money you put into the phone calls and the follow-ups (and mailings if any). That's the minus side of the equation.

Add your speaking fee times the number of gigs that result from your efforts to the plus side of the equation. You will clearly see whether or not your particular equation is viable. Of course, it will change as your business evolves.

You shouldn't expect the equation to be in your favor when you're starting out. The balance should soon start to shift, though. If it doesn't, something needs to be changed.

The benefit of creating an equation is that you extract the emotion out of it. You leave behind any sense of rejection. You silence that small voice that says you'll never be successful. Of course you will be successful. Be good at what you do and then figure out how many phone calls, or connections, you need to make to get the speaking engagements you're looking for. And just keep at it.

Add time for networking and also for continuous improvement in both what you have to offer your clients and in your sales and marketing skills.

Derrick's equation might have been something like this:

10 carefully selected networking events a week (NE)
175 phone calls a week (PC)
5 hours weekly researching potential client databases online (RES)
10 hours weekly follow-up by e-mail, FedEx or phone. (FLWUP)
10 hours weekly improving speaking and marketing skills (ED)

10 NE + 175 PC + 5 HRS RES + 10 HRS FLWUP + 10 ED = 50% deposits for 5 Full paid speaking engagements per month @ $5,000 = $12,500 per month.

Keep in mind this work was divided between two people.

Assuming you're good at speaking and providing value to your client, a dedicated campaign like this is guaranteed success. Derrick went into his speaking profession with full force and he became highly successful after just a few months.

Even a less-dedicated campaign will get you where you want to go, it will just take a little longer.

What's your equation right now? How much time do you dedicate to serious business-generating networking activity? How much time do you dedicate to building your database? How much time do you work the phones to get business?

Is it time to bump it up? In order to become more successful, how will your focus shift?

The truth is, in order to drum up business, one part of your equation needs to be making phone calls. You need to master the art of cold calling.

As a professional speaker, you're often given conflicting advice about cold calls. Should they be part of your marketing methodology? Or not ...

No question about it, warm calls are preferable to cold calls. Still, the best way to warm up a prospect is to make that initial cold call and introduce yourself.

Most speakers need to make cold calls starting out. Even Charles Petty had to do that at first. So did The Referral Coach, Bill Cates, in the beginning.

You will be effective on the phone marketing yourself when you totally and fully believe that you have a compelling message that needs to get out there, and that YOU are the best person to deliver it.

If you call a prospective client with a feeling that you really need the gig or that you are asking for a favor or if you're at all pushy, your results will be dismal.

You CAN get remarkable results from a cold-calling campaign.

Always call with a firm conviction that you are offering a completely unique service and they'd be crazy to say no.

Samantha Ettus, the CEO of Ettus Media Management, a PR firm based in New York City, spends a big chunk of her time working the phones, pitching herself and her clients to people she's never met.

According to the conventional wisdom, that's a big waste of time. A cold call, experts agree, is annoying and an unwanted imposition on busy people. What's more, they say it's inefficient and doesn't bring in much business.

Far better to work through word-of-mouth, networking and established customer contacts. It's the mantra of selling: Spend time building relationships and the deals will follow.

But Ettus's strategy of cold calling has helped her six-person firm land some of its biggest clients. And it remains part of her marketing mix.

Cold calling can work when it's done right. At a time when people are bombarded by pitches via e-mail, direct mail and even instant messaging, a phone call is an extremely personal and effective way of making contact.

It's important to educate yourself on the prospective client before calling. Make sure you qualify them as a good prospect to start out with. Is this firm a good match with your branding and would your topic be a good fit for them?

A phone call with a follow-up e-mail is a good marketing tactic.

Award-winning sales professional, Joe Girard is living proof of the efficacy of cold calling. Girard got in the Guinness World Records for his phenomenal success in selling cars.

He sold 13,000 cars over a period of 15 years. Every day he challenged himself to break his own record.

Joe started out with a phone in the corner of a car dealership and a phone book. The other sales people were not friendly and the sales manager certainly didn't expect much from him. But he didn't know Joe! Joe loves a challenge and the fact that nothing much was expected of him served as fuel.

He tore out a page from the phone book and began phoning total strangers. The rest is history.

As his business grew, Joe used other tactics to bring customers in, by networking and paying referral fees, remembering customers' birthdays and so on.

Girard is now on the speaking circuit where he'll no doubt be as successful as he was selling cars. We can all learn a lot from him.

So get on the phone and start to drum up business. Record everything that transpires during the phone call so that you can follow up effectively. That follow-up phone call is critically important.

Let your prospect know you'll be following up in a couple of weeks and then do so. It often takes five or six phone calls to seal the deal and get the speaking engagement.

How many engagements have you left dangling by not doing a proper follow-up?

How many are still out there sitting on the tarmac? How many have been scooped up by your competition? Resolve in the future to be diligent in your follow-up. Create a system for it.

Have you reached a plateau in your speaking gigs and earning level? Get back on that phone!

You wouldn't drive away leaving money on the road yet speakers, over and over again, walk away from the table with money on it simply because they didn't follow up properly.

Don't wait to have your speech totally written before you start marketing. Just create a good solid marketing blurb to sell your services. When you get your gig, you'll almost certainly have some lead time to polish your speech.

I've sold speeches and courses that I hadn't yet written. It's another way of market testing. If no one was interested in the topic, I didn't write the speech or book.

Begin your sales campaign by building up your database. Quantity is not as important as quality. You don't need thousands of names. One good solid lead is worth a lot!

I suggest narrowing a large database down to the top 100 of those who are most likely to hire you. Those should be the leads that you nurture. Either flag those top 100 hot leads on your database management system or create a simple Word document to track them.

Start by listing former clients, associations that you belong to, and clients your friends have referred you to. Then spread out from there. If you've given a speech at a local pharmaceutical association, then find other branches in other provinces or states. If you've written for an education magazine, find the ad sponsors in that magazine.

While you're at it, create a database for the media as well. If you want to place an article or send out a press release, you'll have your list ready.

Go to friends and colleagues and ask for two different kinds of referrals. Ask your (non-competing) friends to suggest names of organizations that might be a good fit for your speech.

Ask your competing friends if they'd be willing to do a cross-promotion with you, where they recommend you to their former clients for next year's conference and you do the same.

When you follow up on referrals, ask to speak to the convention organizer, meeting planner or special events coordinator.

Once you have them on the phone, tell them you're a professional speaker and ask if they have any events coming up. If you're testing your speech, a monthly meeting is fine although there may not be a budget. Then ask if they've decided on a theme and tell them what you speak about – you'll quickly know whether or not there's a good fit. If it seems appropriate, offer to send them your marketing material to keep in mind for the next meeting.

Then follow up. That follow-up is crucial. The person now knows your name and what you speak about. Call a month or two later to see whether anything else is on the horizon.

This is not a quick-fix process. You need to be in the speaking business for the long haul and you need to be consistent and dedicated. Orvel Ray Wilson, CSP, claims that even a bad selling technique used consistently will out-sell a very polished but inconsistent approach. He's right.

Consistency is the key.

Why not take a few sales training courses to cut down on your learning curve and start out selling at full speed?

A polished consistent sales approach and follow up is an absolutely winning combination.

Remember this is a numbers game. If you make 20 phone calls, youl might get 11 no's, 6 indefinites, 2 possibilities and 1 hot lead. As you build up more referrals and momentum, those numbers will slowly begin to rise in your favor.

The tide has turned!

Keep in mind that Dr. Charles Petty books 100 speeches per year completely by word-of-mouth and his assistant only mails out packages when they're requested. That's what you want to aspire to. And it certainly can be done – however, there's some hard work and total dedication in between.

Book yourself a solid chunk of uninterrupted phone time to make your phone calls. Here are things to remember on the phone:

Always ask if it's a good time to call. Sometimes the answer will be, "Well, I've got ONE minute." And my response is always, "I'll respect that." And I do.

Based on the idea of building a relationship in selling, many people try to get too chummy on a phone call and it works against them. Stay professional. You've got a service to sell, the other person will either want it or not. Chatting simply prolongs a selling process.

Always come from a position of strength rather than scarcity. You've got something great to offer, something that no one else has. And don't take rejection personally. It's a numbers game, that's all.

For those of you who hate to get on the phone and sell, let me say this – it's actually critical to your development, so get over it. You'll get to a point where you won't need to make cold calls. That won't happen until you've worked your way through it and any resistance you have to cold calling.

Mastering cold calling is as important a skill in the speaking business as mastering platform skills.

There are four qualities you need in order to qualify to play the game of marketing yourself as a professional speaker:

- Patience
- Persistence
- Drive
- Focus

Do you have all these qualities?

Which ones need to be more strongly developed?

What's your plan of action in terms of cold-calling?

What's your formula for success?

How many calls in how much time for what results?

How can you build your database?

What's your winning equation?

Are you prepared to do whatever you need to do to drive your speaking career forward?

It's all a numbers game. Make sure you beat the numbers.

CHAPTER 13

Diving In!
with Derrick Sweet

"If at first you don't succeed, skydiving is not for you."
Dan Poynter

Author of three books, Healthy, Wealthy and Wise, Get the Most out of Life and the just-released You Don't Have to Die to Get to Heaven, Derrick Sweet is an excellent speaker whose name is well on its way to becoming a household word.

But everyone has to start somewhere. And Derrick moved from being a financial advisor to being a professional speaker by simply diving right into the deep end.

When he started out, Derrick occasionally spoke without charging. He just wanted to make connections and get himself out there. He spoke free of charge to the Ontario Nurses Association during the Toronto SARS crisis and was rewarded by getting lots of referrals from the engagement.

Derrick took a very circuitous route into the world of professional speaking. When he was 16, he was a pothead and a high school dropout. This created major family stress since his father was with the Royal Canadian Mounted Police.

"One day," he says, "my mother gave me a copy of Wayne Dyer's book, The Sky's the Limit, and it changed the direction of my life. I knew if I wanted to accomplish anything, I had to make some serious changes and so I began working on myself. I starting reading motivational books and got interested in business. I became a stockbroker, although that was always a means to an end and never my end goal."

Derrick began leading seminars on investing with the idea that one day he would lead seminars on the theme of personal development. Finally, after a few years, he was in a financial position to quit his job and that's just what he did. He'd been visualizing himself as a professional speaker and now was the time to take the plunge into the speaking world. He just wanted to get a feel for it, although he still wasn't 100% clear on what he wanted to say.

"My central theme was that human beings have one thing in common," he says. "They all have the desire to make connections with each other."

Derrick came up with a speech outline based on living a healthy, wealthy and wise life. While it wasn't rocket science, it was a good solid theme with a wide appeal to people from many different walks of life.

"As I began speaking," he says, "I got better at it and gained momentum. It may be a cliché, but it's true. If you love what you do, you'll be successful at it. And if you don't love speaking, if you're only in it to attain fame and fortune, get out. It's all about loving people and giving."

It's important to Derrick to build a rapport with the audience. "I'm here to serve and I make that a part of my life," he says. "For example, after every speech that Speakers Gold or other bureaus book for me, I give them referrals so the next time they're recommending a speaker, they'll think of me. Many speakers won't do this and bureaus will begin to lose business because you yourself got the gig and the bureau lost out."

In the first couple of years starting out, Derrick set himself the goal of having 25 conversations with prospective clients each day. When calling companies, he had a simple script that went "Maybe you can help me out. I'm a speaker, who should I speak to about upcoming conferences?" That person was sometimes the head of HR, or a corporate meeting planner. Now Derrick gets enough business from referrals and bureau bookings that he hasn't had to make so many phone calls.

"So many speakers think they're movie stars when they're not," Derrick says. "They're in sales and they have to make those 25 phone calls per day. This is not always a glamorous occupation!"

Derrick also feels it's important that speakers are one with their talk. "Practice it so much that you get reinspired every time you give it," he advises. "I go through my speech – at least four out of eight modules – five days a week. I rehearse my speech in the car on my way to a meeting and as I do, two words might come out that make it grander and tighter. So it continues to evolve. My gut tells me when a new insight is a good one.

"If I get bored rehearsing the speech, I'll do it backwards. I'll do the segments in a different order just to keep it fresh for me. In rearranging it, I sometimes see new openings for greatness."

And nothing less than greatness is what Derrick aspires to. He is well aware that audiences are often jaded and bored. "Today's audiences have the attention span of a fly," he says, "We have to remember we're entertainers as well. It's important to keep people laughing as they learn. My speech is one hour long and there are stories in each module. I refer to Rumi, Christopher Reeve, Thomas Edison. Audience members become inspired when they come into the room and get access to the slumbering powers they didn't know were there."

Derrick personally needs to be inspired when he gives his talk, which is one reason he practices it so often. When he's on the platform, he's not thinking about how he's sounding, he's just giving the speech without having to think or worry about it.

"When I'm practicing, I'm more in my mind than in the spirit of the speech," he says. "I'm thinking a lot about how to break it up or add a story. It's an evolving work of art."

Derrick is also always improving his visual aids which he considers a critical component of his presentation. Derrick speaks about the higher and lower self and just added a cartoon of a man with a devil on one shoulder and an angel on the other. He recommends speakers use visual aids, not as a crutch, but to add to their speech. "For a small fee, you can get as many cartoons as you want from www.animationfactory.com. While PowerPoint is great, don't depend on it," he adds. "If the power is off, you have to go ahead anyway."

Derrick started out in speaking at a modest fee level. He asked for $1,000 for the first couple of months, then as he became more polished, he moved up to $1500 and in another couple of months moved to $3,000 then $5,000. He's now been speaking for about five years. "There are more speakers out there now and fees are an issue," he says. "I've lost a couple of gigs because someone else was cheaper."

Most of Derrick's income comes from selling distributorships in his Healthy Wealthy and Wise company. "In terms of my revenue streams," he says, "I manage my portfolio for an hour every morning. I also get income from book sales and from the Healthy Wealth and Wise Corporation. The two go together because I often get gigs from my distributors. I have one in Memphis who can get me into Cysco and his neighbor is the CEO of FedEx, who now has a copy of my book. Having my own business has been a great way to expand my speaking business."

Derrick firmly believes that success in speaking revolves around having a great attitude. "If qualities such as dedication, perseverance and taking initiative are underdeveloped in you, you can begin to develop them now. Because without them, you'll get nowhere. Hone these skills and you'll reach your dreams."

He has.

To get in touch with Derrick Sweet, go to
www.healthywealthyandwise.com

CHAPTER 14

Pitching From the Platform
Creating and Selling Products

"True discovery consists not in finding new landscapes but in seeing the same landscape with new eyes."

Marcel Proust

Got products to sell? Well, who doesn't? Here's the tough question. What kind of profits are you getting from your sales?

Tens of thousands of professional speakers have products yet only a tiny proportion of that number actually make substantial money from them. For many the cost of the product exceeds the sales revenue. Others make a little money but hardly enough to justify the cost (and the work!) of production.

They make just enough money to think they're doing okay with their product. But when they add in the time they've spent developing and marketing the product, they're actually losing money.

You, as a Six-Figure Speaker, are the exception! Your products are a serious source of revenue that provide solid value to your customers.

There's work involved in setting this up and also a period of trial and error as you market test your product concept. If you're serious about selling products, this work will pay off really well.

Some of the biggest names in Internet marketing, including Joe Vitale, wrote an e-book called The Myth of Passive Income. The main message in the book is that setting up a solid revenue stream based on passive income involves a lot of work.

The setup involves time, money and market smarts. And the result is a fair payoff for all your hard work.

How have you positioned your product? Is your offer compelling? If your copy isn't right on, you'll hurt your sales. If your e-commerce isn't set up properly, you'll also hurt your sales. And if your product is buried on your professional speaking page, few will trouble themselves to resurrect it.

First a caution – don't think in terms of promotion and profit. Don't put your needs ahead of your prospect's needs. Begin by putting yourselves in your customers' or clients' shoes? What do you want from that perspective? Your clients' needs might be different from yours.

As Roxanne Emmerich suggests – let the impetus for product development come from your clients.

To create a profit-generating product, let's look at the steps you'll need to take.

1.   Find an unfilled niche and create a great product with an appealing name that you know your clients want. I started out writing a book about working with bureaus until Ian Percy kindly told me that a speaker had written a book on that topic and it didn't sell well. So I took his sage advice that very day and incorporated my bureau book into my Six-Figure Speaker book. You can fight the marketplace, of course, and occasionally you'll win. But why would you want to? Go with the flow, there's no need to struggle upstream. There are lots of unfilled niches just waiting for you. Go get them!

2.   Write compelling copy from the purchaser's perspective on how this product can help them. Develop a USP – Unique Selling Proposition. Who will buy your product? Why are you the best person to develop it? Define your audience and then pitch to them. Your product should be solving a problem so pitch to the problem and provide the solution.

3. Set up a website dedicated to this product. Keep the name of this site short, memorable, related to the product and easy to spell. Check out www.6figurespeaker.com to see how I've done this.

4.   Give browsers a reason to visit this website. How can you entice visitors? What teaser product can you give web visitors?

5.   Create a golden marketing plan for the website. This might involve banner ads, search engine positioning, reciprocal links, a newsletter or offering something free. Write a couple of articles and send them off to appropriate e-zines for distribution. (Best of all, use Susan Sweeney's brilliant book, 101 Ways to Market Your Website as your bible here. It's easily understandable and contains everything you need to know.)

6. Spend the time and money necessary to promote this website.

7. Once you've made arrangements to take credit card payments online, set up e-commerce with a reliable company, such as Clickbank, Mals e-commerce or PayPal. Your e-commerce site will allow you to sell on your site and also create affiliate links for others who are willing to sell your product. (Caution – surf around until you're sure you're getting the best e-commerce services at the best rate. No point in paying a fortune in

monthly fees if you're just getting started selling products).

8. If you don't know others in your field who would make good affiliates, do a google search on a topic related to your topic. Approach prospects and offer them a review copy of your product to see if they'd like to sell it to the people on their database for a 50% cut.

9. Create an affiliate link just for them and write a compelling letter that they can send out to their clients/customers. The affiliate link allows you to track sales that come from a particular affiliate.

10. Let your newsletter subscribers know of your new product & website.

11. Give them an incentive to buy now. Ask your affiliates to donate one of their products as a bonus giveaway. Or include one of your own products.

12. Monitor and tweak this entire system until it produces the kind of results you're looking for.

Fairly simple, really. And it becomes increasingly simple to add and promote another product once you have your system up and running.

Here's how professional speaker, nurse and business owner Arlene Jorgenson did it. While she was on vacation (often the most productive and creative time), Arlene thought of creating a book called "Everyday Heroes" by collecting inspirational stories that would appeal to a wide range of people.

Nurses would be a great audience for this book and Arlene could create a whole series of books, starting with one called "Everyday Heroes in Healthcare" consisting of stories where nurses shine.

Arlene then thought of having conference attendees record their own stories in a conference room set up for recording. These stories would become the basis for Arlene's book and CD.

Right now, Arlene sells a CD of one of her speeches when she's giving a keynote. Imagine how much better a product with a different angle will do.

Rather than Arlene taking the approach of "Let's make a pile of extra income selling a product" she began by asking herself two questions: Would it be fun to do this and would my clients love it? Yes and yes! If you have these two affirmatives, you know you have a winner.

Writer and speaker Harry van Bommel has a unique spin on creating a new product. "When you're speaking at a conference," he says, "create a setup where conference attendees record their own stories in a tape recorder in the next room. (Hopefully not during your speech!) Those stories, when transcribed, could be an e-book sold to a general audience or given to the conference organizer as a thank you for the event."

Kare Anderson accomplishes the same ends by recording interviews with attendees at a conference and not selling but giving the recording to the meeting planner. It's not a direct revenue maker but the

good will she creates translates into income.
Here are some product possibilities:

- CD/DVD
- Booklet
- Book
- E-book
- Cassette
- Video
- Teleseminar
- Webinar
- Audit/Assessment
- Conference Feedback in a CD
- Newsletters
- Home Study Courses
- MP3 Downloads
- Membership Site
- Software

What added service in the form of a product could you provide your clients?

Criteria: Your product has to have a broad appeal and a great name. It has to either command a good price or if it's a lower priced item, have the potential for massive sales.

And look back at the title of this chapter. Pitching from the Platform. DON'T. Please. Not when you've got a paying gig. I've heard lots of complaints about speakers getting a great fee for a speaking engagement and pitching product shamelessly on the client's dime. Don't attach your name to that.

If you're good on the platform and have a great product, it will sell at the back of the room. Audience members tend to want to take a little piece of you home with them.

Audio Products

With today's audience, CDs are often big sellers. If you have a speech, you have an article and you also have a CD or DVD.

Get a series of CDs professionally recorded with a well designed cover and sell those at the back of the room after your speech. You can also sell these on your website. In fact, you can now record yourself as you're speaking directly onto a CD. You can then edit it to take out any rough edges and you've got a great product to sell. Producing and selling CDs really expands your horizons.

One thing you can do with any of your products is pre-sell them to the convention organizer who's hired you to give the keynote address. You might want to offer a bulk discount price so that each audience member has a CD, newsletter or book of yours. You're getting your products out there, the organizer is getting a good deal and everyone's happy.

Make arrangements with your client to have your speech taped, then have that tape professionally edited, burned onto a CD and packaged. This could be your first product. You might want to add a question and answer segment to the CD. You'll need permission for most music that you want to use as a background. Or you can download music from the website: http://www.royaltyfreemusic.com

Your CD production cost could run anywhere from $500 to $8,000 so do a market survey of your audience members and colleagues to make sure that there is interest in your topic. These CDs can do double duty as demos for bureaus and prospective clients.

Affiliating with others who have credible e-commerce websites and a large database of prospective clients will increase your sales. It's typical to give an affiliate half of your fee so if your e-book sells for $97, your affiliate normally gets half of that sum. These are sales you wouldn't have made on your own and it costs you nothing so 50% is perfectly reasonable in these cases.

E-Courses

Increasing sales through e-courses is easy. You simply create anywhere from seven to 10 lessons plans. Then write your copy. Who would benefit from taking this course and why? List the benefits, add some client testimonials, add a bonus for signing up now and send out an e-mail announcing your new e-course to your database.

If you've got a good database and you've created a compelling offer, you'll do well with this.

What people are really paying for is your personal time. Otherwise, they could simply read your information in a book. The selling point of e-courses is that you personally will review their materials and help make them as appealing as possible – and you'll do it for much less than your hourly coaching fee.

If you seriously want to explore e-courses, go to: www.hypnotic-products/ebooks.html

Scroll down to the e-book on making money from e-courses.

Teleconferences

Teleconferences are another source of income if you've got a valuable message to impart. Assuming you have an online database with permission to send e-mails, you can send an e-mail announcing a new teleconference.

Often experts in the field offer a free teleconference session in order to get ongoing clients. They tell their clients upfront, "I'll be sharing information with you for 45 minutes of this call – do you mind if I then add a five-minute pitch for my services?" You'll have to experiment to find what works best for you and your audience. Personally, I feel you should charge for a teleconference call and also get clients from the call. It works for me.

For free information on how to set up a conference call, go to: www.prosperityplace.com/teleclass/inst.html or to purchase an e-book on the subject, go to: www.greatteleseminars.com

You can subscribe to a no-cost teleconference service at www.freeconferencecall.com. The only downside to this service is that there's no operator if you have any problems on the call. Otherwise, it's a great service provided you have fewer than 100 participants.

You can subscribe to a paid service at: www.greatteleseminars.com

Teleconference calls need to be interactive. Again, what people are paying for is not just your information but answers to their questions.

Becoming a Merchant

The first step toward maximizing your income with products is to get your own merchant number so that you can sell your self-published book and/or other products directly by accepting credit cards. This allows you to take advantage of the impulse sale and most sales are based on impulse. Ask your local bank to send you an application form.

Use a merchant service to sell your products online. The services I recommend are:

- www.clickbank.com
- www.paypal.com
- www.mals-e.com

See which of these services works best for you. The benefit of mals-e.com is that you only need to add a button to your website rather than a script which is a little more complicated. Make sure you read all the fine print before making a decision as to which service is right for you.

Until your website is up and running, marketed well and listed in all the search engines and until you've created a publicity campaign for your product, your sales will be low so it doesn't make sense to use a merchant and shopping cart service that charges a hefty monthly fee. Start out with one of the services listed above and later when you need to bump up, you'll be getting enough sales to justify the expense for a more sophisticated service.

When approaching a financial organization for your offline merchant card, you'll be glad you took the time to develop a well-thought-out business plan since the bank will want to know all about your business before offering you a merchant card.

And the rules for accepting the major credit cards by phone are very different from accepting cards online. Negotiate with your service provider for the best terms and lowest possible discount rate.

Pricing Products

Once you have products, you need a formula for pricing them. You should have a discount price for bulk orders from corporate clients who are also hiring you to give a keynote and another price for individuals who are buying directly from you. The rule of thumb in determining price is that it should be five times your cost.

Often one of the organizers of the group you're speaking to will offer to help you with book or other product sales. You can also ask the person who introduces you to the audience to mention that you'll be available afterwards to sign your books or sell your tapes.

How important are products? Well, according to speaker and time-management expert, Harold Taylor, they're very important. Product sales comprise 90% of Taylor's business and speaking only 10%.

Being in time management is a plus since Taylor's products are of interest to each member in his audience and those who purchase then go on his database for follow-up catalogs and other promotions.

While product sales in Harold Taylor's case represent a major chunk of his income, other speakers use products more to increase name recognition than to add to income. You find the formula that suits your needs best.

"If a speaker doesn't have audio programs and books to sell at their engagements or on the Internet," says Jack Zufelt, author of The DNA of Success, "they are leaving tens of thousands of dollars on the table.

Jack learned to make those kinds of products in a matter of days not years. "It's easy when you know how," he says. "It doesn't take a polished salesperson to move product from the stage. It takes a great presentation. Product moves at the back of the room if you are a good presenter. I sometimes forget to mention my book and tapes but I consistently sell between 40 and 100% of my audience. That puts an additional $5,000 to $30,000 in my pocket each time I speak. One of the most profitable sources of cash flow is through selling my book."

- What products are you in the process of developing?
- What innovative approach can you take to the marketplace?
- What products would be a good fit with your branding and central message?

Fix a timeline to the answers to these questions and then begin to create a step by step process to reaching your goal.

Product sales should certainly be a good solid source of income for every speaker and a product development strategy needs to be a component of your business plan.

CHAPTER 15

The Famous Author Syndrome
Writing and Publishing Your Book

"The worth of a book is what you can carry away from it."
James Bryce

Most speakers feel they need to have published a book. They sometimes feel they need the book before they get out there speaking. That is putting the cart before the horse.

Do you feel you're nobody until you've written a book? Well, let me see. If you don't have enough to offer right now just as you are, writing a book won't really help. There are many highly successful speakers who don't have and don't want a book.

Start by getting out there. Get your speeches and your initial product in circulation. It won't be perfect but it's a beginning. You'll learn from the experience as you go.

The truth is that books are rarely moneymakers. They make great keys, though. Books will open doors for you and add to your credibility. You can often raise your fees once you've written a book. So if you're planning to write a book, go right ahead.

This is not just an exercise in vanity, though. Don't write a book to promote your career. Write a book because you have something of value to say.

You know your topic and area of expertise so do a great spin on that. Play with your idea until you know you've taken it as far as it will go. Then plan your book, beginning with a mission statement and a brief chapter by chapter outline.

The process varies for different writers. For me, it all starts with a great title that ignites my imagination. Once I have that, everything starts to coalesce around it. I now know exactly what belongs in that book. I also know what doesn't. Often writing consists more of editing the information you already have than it does actually creating something new. Know what belongs in your book and what should stay on the cutting floor.

Once you've written a book, you need to decide whether to go after a publisher or to self-publish. Going after a publisher is a process that, in itself, can be every bit as daunting as the writing.

You find a list of agents and publishers and then choose the ones that seem the best fit. You send your perfect proposal out and wait. And wait and wait. Most publishers don't like simultaneous submissions. In other words, they like to think they're the only ones reviewing your work. And they may take a few weeks to get back to you. So you submit to one publisher at a time.

Unless, of course, you have connections in the publishing world which is always helpful. There are real benefits to being published by an independent publisher. Their distribution system is great. They can reach bookstores that often not receptive to a self-published book. Also some periodicals won't review self-published books. So credibility is a huge factor here.

There's more than credibility at stake. While you get to keep the profits you make from self-publishing, without a wide distribution system, there often aren't any profits. And if there are, frequently they trickle in over a period of five years.

I needed an outside publisher for the history book, Life of a Loyalist: Tales of Old Nova Scotia that I wrote.   There was no way I could personally distribute that book.

Altitude Publishing accepted my proposal and published the book. However, I have self-published two of my marketing books because I have my own audience for them. And I have no patience for the waiting game – waiting for approval, waiting for the cover design – and having no control over the process.

I recommend that you explore both options to see which is right for you. Outside publishers often take weeks to respond to your query. On the other hand, I had an instant response from Robert Reed who published this book - www.rdrpublishers.com.

Take a tip from author and speaker Lance Secretan, who self-published a wonderful book called One: The Art and Practice of Conscious Leadership.

Many authors still have thousands of copies of their book languishing in the basement. But not Lance. An astute businessman, he pre-sold 200 copies of his book to 500 colleagues around the world and ended up with one of the largest print runs in Canada that year.

How did he do that? You know, I haven't asked. Frankly, I'd rather not know. I prefer to think of the many ways he could have done it, and then see what I can come up with on my own. I think it was actually quite simple.

The way I would do it is to put out an offer to everyone in my database, offering to sell bulk book orders at just a little over cost. The trick is to have a good list. This is a constant theme throughout this book. The trick to getting gigs, selling products and making great connections is to have a good list!

However Lance did it, you can be sure that one of the critical elements was having his own list of colleagues and fans and an excellent relationship with his subscribers.

It's a great way to have your book become a best seller before it's even gone to print!

If you decide to self-publish, you'll need the specs for the book so printers can quote you a price on the printing. You'll need the name of the book, quantity of copies, size, number of pages and so on. The website www.booksjustbooks.com will give you more information on asking for a quote.

Here's what I used to request a quote from different printers. Feel free to adapt it for your own purposes.

REQUEST FOR QUOTE
Book Cover Size: 5.5 x 8.5
Spine: ½ inch
Pages: 200
Stock: 60 lb. matte offset
Cover Stock 10 pt. Cornwall with .5 mil plastic lamination outside only.
Black ink.
Four color process cover
Quote for print copies of 2,000 and 5,000

You'll need an ISBN number for your book. You can get that free of charge in Canada by calling 819-994-6872 or filling out a form online at www.collectionscanada.ca. In the U. S., go to www.ISBN.org for information. The price in the U. S. is $225 to $350 for the number.

You'll want to register your book with www.bowkerlink.com. Once you complete their registration form, your book will be listed in the catalog of all registered books in print.

If you plan to have your books sold through any retail stores, you'll need a barcode on the back cover. It's called an EAN-3 code and the printer will put it on the book for a small extra charge or you can purchase the software and create it yourself. Go to www.creatbarcodes.com to get the software.

To get your book listed on www.amazon.com, go to the website, join the Advantage program and fill out the registration form. It will take up to two weeks for the application to be approved. Once it is, upload a jpg of your book cover on the site and mail Amazon copies of your book to send out to purchasers. How simple is that?

Place your book in as many categories as possible so that when buyers search Amazon by typing in key words your book title comes up.

Writing an e-book can be a little simpler than a print book. E-books are usually shorter with more white space and less text than a print book. E-books need to be well-designed so create the book with the Adobe PDF program by going to www.adobe.com and either buying or trying their program to put your document into a PDF format.

The e-books that sell well are how-to books that you can download immediately to get the information you need, although Chris Widener had huge success with his fictional e-book The Angel Within.

Go to www.fabjobs.com and purchase one of their books to see a great example of how an e-book is done. Readers should be able to surf through your e-book. My e-book Speaking for Money has 100 websites that online readers can click on to get more information on a particular topic.

If writing a book seems like a huge challenge, you can go to www.idictate.com where you can dictate your book on the website and it will be transcribed and the transcript e-mailed back to you so you can clean it up and create your book.

E-books can command a higher price than print books. If I sell a book online, I can create a compelling sales piece to go right along with it, just as though the browser has a sales person right on their shoulder. That sales piece can create a mystique around the book and browsers can't peak inside the book the way they would in a bookstore. That creates even more mystery so they buy the book.

As an added incentive, I could ask my colleagues to contribute their products and services and create a special one-time offer. Those purchasing this book within a twenty-four hour period would receive bonuses with a value that is much more than the book price.

What do my colleagues get in return? Publicity and an introduction to a whole new group of prospective clients or customers. Not a bad trade-off.

Even though e-books can be more lucrative, I personally am addicted to print. I like a tangible product.

Final advice on publishing a book: Wait until you really have something solid to say and then do your research on publishing and self-publishing options to see which would work best for you. An e-book can work well if you're set up for e-commerce. Otherwise stick to print.

And a book WILL NOT, I repeat, create a career for you. It will open doors.

CHAPTER 16

Differentiate or Die!
with Donna Long, CSP

"I owe my success to having listened respectfully to the very best advice and then going away and doing the exact opposite."

G. K. Chesterton

Donna Long has an urgent message for you. If you want to reach the next level in your speaking career, you must differentiate yourself! You've got to stand out and be memorable if you want to get booked over and over again.

Donna created a twist in her marketing materials and in her programs that not only make her stand out but also increase her value to her clients.

What sets Donna apart is that she uses Rock and Roll to emphasize her message and her sessions are always extremely interactive and a lot of fun.

When she wanted to make the transition from workshops into keynotes, the change happened very gradually. While she's been in business for 16 years, she's only been doing the music since 1999.

Donna's background is with the Disney Corporation and she always included music in the presentations she gave there, so it was natural for her to continue to use music in her keynote presentations.

Everything escalated once she and her partner started using classic rock and roll music to anchor their corporate messages. They crafted a speech called "The Jukebox Journey."

One day, a friend and Donna were reminiscing about oldies and they said to each other, "Why don't we get serious about writing a book about this?" "I threw myself into it and spent a year finding a major record company who would work with us," says Donna. "We finally found someone with EMI Capital Records in their special markets division. EMI agreed to create a 21-song CD of original oldies just for our company. You can't buy it anywhere else. I made dozens of phone calls and he was the first guy to take my call, the others I couldn't get through to. It was a fluke. I called late in the evening and the guy at EMI picked up the phone himself. We chatted and I was very enthusiastic and he responded to that enthusiasm."

It's a matter of being in the right place at the right time. It's also about being persistent.

Donna and her partner were so excited that they wrote and published their first book Rock Your Way to Happiness. It was a personal self-help book rather than business so they decided to write a second book which focused more on business called Jukebox Journey to Success.

Donna and her partner Al noticed that whenever their office staff presented proposals including the musical concept they had a much better response. Corporations wanted something different and they differentiated themselves from their competition.

The music lends itself to making the sessions highly interactive. "I have a conga line and a hand jive contest," says Donna. "If people don't remember that, they at least remember seeing it in Grease. I bring six people onstage, teach the audience how to hand jive and let them vote on their favorite, then give that person a prize. There's always a serious lesson connected to the hand jive."

When she needs to, Donna can also be serious. Her most requested speech is called "The Spirit of Leadership, Preparing for the Emerging Workforce" about what to expect between now and 2020 and how to prepare for the coming changes, based on the Hudson Institute Research. The keynote involves data and guidance on what businesses need to do to prepare for this emerging workplace.

"My speech is interactive to the point where we're out of our chairs every 10 to 15 minutes," says Donna. "By threading music and fun into the keynote, the audience is rejuvenated and really listening to stuff rather than nodding off. It's a blend of solid content and fun with interactivity intertwined. And it's not a tough sell at all."

As a handout for their keynotes, Donna gives out a CD card that looks like a card cut in the shape of a jukebox. As you open the greeting card, there's a puppet that the CD fits into. Donna uses the client's logo on the CD, along with an acronym that is tied to three or four points that she makes in the keynote. Many organizations consider these the most creative handouts they've ever had. They certainly don't get left in the seats!

The music that Donna uses in her keynotes is also in the CD. Along with the CD, Donna provides attendees with a standard PowerPoint handout with three or four points that are all connected to one of the songs. So when they put the CD in their car, they're reminded of some of the messages in the keynote.

"Here's a neat story about how effective it all can be," says Donna.

"One of my first major contracts was with Daytona International Speedway in Daytona Beach.   I was involved with one of the colleges there and the president of Daytona International Speedway asked the manager of the business institute if he could find a consultant for customer service training of 1,200-1,500 employees. The trainer would spend two hours with 200-300 employees at a time. Only two hours. 'And I want it to be meaningful training.' the president added."

Quite a challenge!

So Donna met with him and proposed using the Beach Boys "Good Vibrations" as an anchor. She then used the acronym of VIBES to anchor the lesson.   V – visual appearance, had to look professional, I - immediate service – interact with guest at speedway – B - body language, E - eye contact, S - smile.   She tied these basic customer service fundamentals to a song, then she did a little game show for two hours showing pictures of good and bad behavior with the game show and the music.

"Speedway had the acronym printed up on a sticker which was pasted behind everyone's name tag," says Donna. "The employees still have them and still play 'Good Vibrations' often. Every employee is reminded of five training fundamentals every time they hear it."

This was a short two-hour training program with an audience of 300. Donna normally wouldn't do training under those constraints, but she ended up having great fun and Speedway was thrilled with the results. "That's an example of how I use music to ground my message," says Donna. "Music is used as a memory anchor for real solid lessons and research confirms that this strategy is very effective."

Recently Donna opened a meeting on leadership with the song "Put a Little Love in your Heart".   "Leaders need more heart so we gave them a little bit of soul for their meeting," she says. "They enjoyed it and we're currently negotiating another series of meeting openers with them."

Donna and her partner are also producing other training videos based on the same concept.   They continue to get requests from customers for keynotes or customized training. Sometimes customers will call with something specific in mind, then they try to find music that ties in with what they want.

"I hope we can continue to use the music and do other things like game shows. I find it difficult to do a keynote without interaction. It doesn't really engage the audience," Donna claims. "The rock and roll music makes me more memorable and that's often just what the client wants. We appeal to the client who looks for a non-traditional type of presentation."

In the future, she plans to use the same strategy with a focus on Customer Relationship Management.   She will also do more training online so she's not traveling as much as she has been in the past few years.

Donna's plans for her future are a good reminder that our goals and intentions need to be re-evaluated regularly since they tend to change over time.

You can bet that no matter what direction Donna Long decides to turn in, music will continue to be a part of her winning equation and so will being memorable.

Donna can be reached at www.learningjourneyinc.com or www.jukeboxlearning.com.

CHAPTER 17

Stay Connected to Your Power Source

"It is always with excitement that I wake up in the morning wondering what my intuition will toss up to me, like gifts from the sea. I work with it and rely on it. It's my partner."

Jonas Salk

When marketing guru Dan Kennedy listened to a news broadcast about a hurricane, he stopped dead in his tracks as the weatherman said, "As the center of the storm moved inland, it began losing strength. As the hurricane moved away from its power source - the warm waters of the Atlantic – it starting losing steam."

It suddenly struck Dan that this is why so many entrepreneurs (and speakers) are able to reach a certain level of success which then declines.

They've moved away from their power source.

Initially they were happy with the success they achieved and then they began to coast. Soon they just drifted away from the very foundation that made them successful.

They stopped being vigilant. They stopped looking for and adapting to the changes in an ever-evolving marketplace. Or sometimes when they were doing well, they changed their business model and moved away from their power source.

Adaptation is the key.

Years ago, I went to boarding school with a young woman who was the women's log-rolling champion of the world. At the time, I thought that was bizarre and I never got to know her. Now I think that she was brilliantly suited to today's world. Keep those feet moving, watch the weather changes, maintain your balance and always be connected to your core body strength and your intuition which is the source of your power. I suspect whatever this woman is doing now, she's doing well. What great skills to have!

When I was taking presentation-skills training a few years back, I was videotaped during a practice speech. Watching the tape later at home was a humbling experience. I had a strong opening and a powerful ending but in the middle, I simply went flat. It was as though I simply pulled the plug in the middle. Just pulled out my connection to my source.

Being disconnected, it seems, was my default mode at the time.

Once I was aware of that disconnection, I worked to correct it and now, when I'm giving a speech, I watch the audience. If I notice any sense of distraction on their part, I reinfuse my speech with energy and enthusiasm.

My goal is to be plugged in to my source. All the time.

What is your power source? What is your area of brilliance, something only you can do, something you are 100% passionate about? Once you've carefully analyzed and defined that source, be vigilant about staying plugged in to it.

It's easy to lose your connection if you're tired or stressed. Part of your job as a speaker is to make sure that you take good care of yourself, whatever that means to you, so that you're always in top form onstage.

At the National CAPS Conference, Suzie Humphreys got up and gave her speech "I Can Do That!" I wasn't drawn by the title so Suzie had to win me over and she did that the minute she began.

Suzie was so connected to her source, she was absolutely radiant on the stage and clearly having a great time. So was the audience.

Part of her secret was that Suzie was herself. No posturing, no pretending, no bending to fit whatever mold she thought the audience wanted. Nothing fake. Suzie was the real deal.

And it was a brilliant performance. It was a joy to see and hear.

No surprise that Suzie, when addressing an NSA convention, got the longest standing ovation in history. We automatically know when someone is connected. We also know it's not all that common. And strangely, we too, begin to feel connected.

When I spoke to her recently, I said, "Suzie, you were right in the zone." She responded, "And it was so easy!"

That's what being connected to your source means – it's effortless. It's energizing rather than draining.

Remember a time when you were in the zone. What was going on at the time?

How can you recreate that every time you're onstage?

What does it take for you to be in the zone?

It looks simple. It is simple. But it's rare for a speaker to be fully in their power onstage. It takes a lot of backstage work. You need to know yourself very well and you need to fully accept all aspects of your personality – the good, the bad and the indifferent.

You also have to be crystal clear on why you're on the platform and why your message is important for others to hear.

That foundation of self-knowledge combined with caring about your audience will ensure you're always connected to your source and you will not only blow your audiences away, you'll walk away refueled and re-energized rather than drained.

That's exactly the goal you want to aim for. When you're refuelled and energized after your speech, so is your audience and they'll soon have you back for a return engagement.

Your connection with your source is a connection well worth cultivating.

CHAPTER 18

If the Shoe Doesn't Fit....
with Dr. Charles Dygert, CSP

"You become your question."
Anthony Robbins

One thing Dr. Charles Dygert has learned in his years of experience as a professional speaker is that it's the best job in the world when you meet your client's expectations. And it's the worst when you don't.

"It's an ideal engagement for me when someone hires me after hearing me speak. They know exactly what I do and know just what to expect the next time around." he says.

"Every now and then, maybe once out of 30 engagements, someone hires me who hasn't heard me speak and then says, 'Well, that wasn't exactly what we were looking for.'"

He finds it frustrating. He's written three books and is an excellent communicator. In his agreement, he states very clearly what he does and what audiences can expect but still finds that occasional client who is left scratching his head.

I can relate. I'll sometimes have someone come up to me after my seminar saying, "I thought this was about presentation skills, not about marketing." No matter how clear you are, people tend to see what they expect.

Dr. Dygert does his due diligence well before he delivers the speech. He customizes each speech by asking the client beforehand. "What are the demographics of your audience? Who is attending? What four outcomes do you want?"

Often the client doesn't really know. Dr. Dygert, a professor who teaches in the MBA program at Franklin University in Ohio wonders, "How do you communicate to someone who hasn't heard you speak precisely what you're going to do? I'm a type A and like to be very accurate."

He much prefers speaking for a client who's already heard him and who is 100% clear on what exactly his message is.

For 15 years, Dr. Dygert used to do roughly 125 speeches a year. The fact that he is a pilot and flew himself to many of his engagements made the travel a little less onerous. Even so, it was a demanding schedule.

"I gave a speech in January at Long Island, New York City," he says. "I had to finish precisely at noon so I could fly to Phoenix for another speech the next morning. It took me a week to recover! It's the only way I could have done it at the time. The benefit of speaking so frequently is that it keeps you really sharp and at the top of your game."

Dr. Dygert now finds that giving 30 to 40 keynotes a year, along with his teaching, keeps him as busy as he wants to be.

Much like Dr. Charles Petty, Dr. Dygert's marketing campaign was almost solely word of mouth. "I really didn't have to market, not even at the start of my speaking career. I was always so busy and just kept getting busier. My reputation always preceded me and I got lots of referrals."

One of the secrets of his phenomenal success is to leave people with something they'd never heard before that they could apply to improve their lives.

His final word of advice to professional speakers is to make sure the speaking engagement is a good fit for you, and not to be afraid to turn it down if it isn't. If it doesn't seem right for you, chances are, it's not your audience.

"If I had to do it over again, I would turn down more gigs," he says. "I've discovered that you never want to talk to a group of attorneys about human relations. They're not interested! There are some organizations and audiences, I won't speak to anymore."

It's not one bit gratifying, he now realizes, to speak to an audience you know will never implement your message. He's discovered his toughest audience is an all–male audience so now he hires a woman to share the platform with him. That works well to cut down on the competitive alpha male atmosphere he used to encounter.

Experience is the best teacher in the end.

Dr. Dygert can be reached at www.dygert.com

CHAPTER 19

The Full-Tilt Speaker
with Chris Widener

"If you don't blow your own horn, someone else will use it as a spittoon."

Anonymous

Rather than taking slow cautious steps and building up a career over a period of years by taking on free speaking engagements, Chris Widener went full tilt into professional speaking.

Actually, it never dawned on him to start out by speaking for free. He started out by writing columns on the Internet that were driving qualified people to his website, which was the whole point. His strategy worked very well. When he was first asked to speak, he began by asking for $3,500 per speech and then moved up to $4,500, and when a company offered him $6,000, he moved to that figure. Now he charges $8,000 for a one-hour keynote.

Chris gets lots of bookings at that fee. "A modern speaker has to consider themselves as an information provider and speaking is only one venue of providing that information," he says. "My income is distributed quite nicely across products, writing, and speaking."

His product sales alone provide a healthy income. "My products are doing very well," he says. "My latest product just got sold to Costco and Sam's Club – we'll be rolling out 27,000 units this month. We developed three boxed sets, a leadership box and a personal development for women box and a sales box. Each box consists of 14 CDs and one DVD. We licensed content from the world's top speakers and included their CDs in the box. We left each speaker's contact info on their CD. The boxed set includes Brian Tracy, Zig Ziglar, Naomi Rhodes - all the big-name speakers.

"We approached Costco and Sam's Club and they made their first purchase. We're hoping to eventually sell 30,000 units a month. I could live on that alone if I chose to."

When asked why, with so much income from product, he continues to take on speaking engagements, Chris's answer was quick.

"Why do the speaking? Well, at NSA meetings, it fascinates me how much discussion there's been about whether you want to speak or prefer to sit in your underwear and make money. We're the speaker's organization, not the Internet marketing association! I speak because I love the one-on-one and audience interaction. Theoretically, I could choose to never leave my house again, quit my speaking, and continue to develop personal development stuff, getting a multi-book deal with a publisher and so on. Here's the thing that keeps me speaking: it's important and it changes people's lives."

Chris's latest book is called The Angel Inside, a short fictional account of a man who goes to Italy and, on the last afternoon of vacation, he meets little old man who teaches him important life lessons.

"We just did a second print run of 25,000. I self-published and the book has done well. Now a publisher is interested in picking up the rights to this book and doing a series based on it. I've always self-published and made good money on it. The only reason I'm gong with a traditional publisher is for the credibility. If you have a distribution channel, you're better off self-publishing and keeping the revenues yourself. One of the secrets to my high book sales is that my website gets 5 million hits a year."

Visit Chris's website at www.madeforsuccess.com to see why he gets so much traffic.

Chris attributes his incredible success to a "mixture of things that no one will ever be able to pour into a beaker and look at. Success comes from chutzpah, timing, luck, hard work, location, partnerships, relationships, sacrifice. All sorts of things. The most important factor is your ability to influence people, whether buyers, partners or clients."

Chris believes that the speaker who has more influence over people will do better in the marketplace. It's not only his belief, it's his main speech – "The Secrets of Influence" – and the first thing he learned when he started speaking.

When Chris's coach saw his first video, he said, "You're one of the best speakers I've seen, but it really doesn't matter. Many people who aren't as good do well because they're marketing better. So that's what you need to do." It was good advice and Chris acted on it. "If I can't connect with that buyer," Chris says, "they're gong to pick someone else."

As for what he does to connect with the buyers, Chris says it boils down to "two things: I listen to the client and then reframe it and give it back to them. If I can't meet their needs in a very successful way, I say I'm not your guy. I stick to what I do best. If I can hit the ball out of the park, I'll say here's what I can do for you. Listening is the most important."

The second thing that's important is positioning.

"Lots of speakers need to position themselves properly in the marketplace. I began to think about the ton of older speakers who are wildly successful – Dennis Waitley, Zig Ziglar, Brian Tracy and Mark Sanborn.   They made millions on the platform and I couldn't compete with them.   What I could do, though, is position myself to be in the next generation. I asked myself 'Who's next?' and then I decided to be #1 in the next generation."

How Chris managed to pull this off was a minor miracle in itself. One of his success secrets is his careful strategizing before he makes a move.   He wanted to position himself with some of the world's top speakers. They didn't know (or care) who he was and what he had to offer. So what did he do? He took an enormous huge leap. And it paid off.

He decided to position himself with John Maxwell, author of The 21 Irrefutable Laws of Leadership, by hosting a conference and hiring him to be the primary keynote speaker. Chris was planning to emcee and also be a speaker at the conference. In order to afford Maxwell's $40,000 speaking fee, he had to take out a line of credit using his house as collateral. He rented the largest auditorium in Seattle, Washington, put on this huge conference and lost his shirt to the tune of $30,000.

So the venture was a bust, right? Wrong!

"But ... I became friends with John Maxwell and his organization," says Chris, "and have since done about $200,000 worth of business with him. In essence, I bought a relationship with him. In other words, I had to put out some money and risk some capital if I wanted to play with the big boys. I'm not sure if that venture was a sign of guts or stupidity. Before I decided to go ahead with this venture, I asked my wife what if only four people show up? What if we don't sell one ticket? We'll lose $100,000. And she said 'Okay, we can live with that. Let's do it.'"

Four speakers spoke at the event.   Lombardi, Whittaker and Maxwell spoke along with Chris who also hosted the day.   350 people showed up. It was a relatively low turn-out because the ticket price was high. Still, it all turned out to be very worthwhile.

"There are different ways to position yourself with others," says Chris. "Sometimes you have to pony up some money. Basically I bought Maxwell's time which gave me opportunity to spend time with him."

It's created an ongoing relationship. Maxwell has now started a speaker's bureau with only 15 speakers. Chris is one of them.

"I'm the cheapest on the roster." says Chris. "The only reason I was asked was because I had a relationship with his organization. In the last two years, they've booked me 15 times at $8,000 a pop. I've done a quarter of a million dollars worth of business with him over the last few years by putting things together and hosting conference calls and so on."

Chris's positioning strategy worked out amazingly well in the long term. Jim Rohn International just took over Chris's business and is selling and distributing his products. It's been a very lucrative arrangement for both parties.

"They have a wider distribution than I have and they've got a great name. Jim won the Masters of Influence Award in Phoenix in July. He has incredible contacts; he is an absolute master of promotion. He put on a conference in Los Angeles for 1,300 people. There were 20 nations represented for this three-day event."

"I just emceed an event for Jim Rohn, Brian Tracey and Dennis Waitley. They asked me to emcee because they've seen me speak and host these things. At the event, I put a video camera on them and got glowing endorsements from all of them.

"On camera, Brian Tracey said, 'I've given over 3,000 presentations around the world and never seen anyone better than Chris.' Dennis said, 'Chris is one of the great new names on the international scene.' And Jim Rohn has personally endorsed me by saying, 'Chris is the leader of a new generation of personal development speakers and authors.' It positions me great. Sometimes you have to invest money and take a risk to get those kinds of returns."

The returns have been more than Chris ever dreamed of. He was part of Jim Rohn's 'One Year Success Plan'. Chris was the featured contributing editor for the written material and contributed an article in every week's lesson. He also hosted all the conference calls.

Chris's strategy to position himself as number one in the second generation of speakers has worked phenomenally well. "These big name speakers called me with a need and I helped them," he says. "After working with them, they came to me and said that they saw my potential. Since then we've done many projects and events together."

As for the future, Chris would like to sign a deal with a traditional publishing house, create a best-selling book and raise his speaking fees so he can pick and choose his speaking engagements. He'd also like to build the personal development library that he's currently distributing himself and move it to an MP3 digital distribution model."

After all that, he's got his eye on the senate.

"I want to make a difference in the world. After watching five minutes of the evening news, I realize we need leaders who can help navigate the waters of the world. If not me, who? I feel compelled; I have a great life, I'm only 38 years old. If I position my life properly, I'd like to be able to serve in that way."

Chris is always up for taking on something new. He was struck by Tony Robbins question, 'What drives you?" and gave some thought to his answer.

"Adventure drives me – I love a good adventure. If it's fun and interesting, sign me up for it. Some speakers hate traveling, but for me, airports are adventures and as long as it's an adventure, I'm happy. I get to hunt and look around somewhere new. I'm driven by the pleasure principle."

Finally, he says, "Speaking is a real fortunate business to be in.

Imagine making great money, having loads of fun and helping so many people. We are so lucky in this part of the world. We should be thankful everyday for opportunities and use them well."

Speakers would do well to emulate Chris's career path. It all started with a vision which he refused to relinquish, even when common sense told him he should. He knew better.

Hang on to your vision no matter what!

Chris Widener can be reached at www.madeforsuccess.com

CHAPTER 20

Your Business Machine
with Mark Ellwood

"All great leaders have vision and idealization in which they can continually imagine the perfect outcome to all situations."
Brian Tracy

Mark Ellwood takes a very practical approach to the business of speaking, writing and consulting. The key to his success is that he turns his goals into reality.

Mark believes that all speakers need to thoroughly understand their business machine and be clear about how they're going to generate and sustain income from speaking, consulting and training. In other words, they have to know where the money is.

"If referrals are the best income-generator, then the focus should be on the referral machine, if it's repeat business, make that work well." says Mark. "Avoid activities that don't contribute to the machine."

Mark also recommends that you ask established speakers how they did it. In his case, he did it the hard way, spending years slugging it out by doing freebies in Rotary Clubs and so on until he gradually built up a base of paying clients.

And that's one way to go – the route of sheer persistence. It's a well-worn path, you'll get there eventually and you'll have lots of company on the way.

"A faster model is to put your resources – time and money – into the areas that give you the highest return," Mark claims. "If that means producing a video, brochure, business card, then that's exactly what you need to do."

Mark suggests that if you get the highest return from making phone calls or speaking for free, then that's where you need to invest your time. Or if writing an article for a publication that reaches your target audience gets returns for you, that's where you need to focus.

And he's a big fan of delegating anything that has to be done, but not necessarily by you!

"Spend time on your highest activities and less time on administrative activities. Filing or cleaning your office or invoicing and sending out packages are activities you need to delegate to someone else."

One way that successful speakers can save a great deal of time is by automating, eliminating or delegating administrative tasks. Mark recommends using contact automatic response systems so that one article or proposal out can be sent out simultaneously to a bunch of prospects with an automatically scheduled follow-up.

"It takes more time initially to set that up but consider that you're investing in training. You have to think down the road," he says. "Some people are inherently good planners with the ability to think ahead, see the outcome and think of the intermediate steps. If you don't have that ability, you need to create a system to help you do that kind of planning."

Write down your goals along with a timeline and then work backwards to create a daily to-do list. Make sure that your to-do list is achievable or you'll always feel that somehow you've failed to accomplish your goals.

"Break your big projects into small manageable pieces so that you don't feel overwhelmed," says Mark. "That way, you'll have evened the playing field with those who are naturally well organized."

"In our research, we find the one thing people claim to want to do less of is watching television," says Mark. "How can you turn that time into a higher priority time?"

Don't get so caught up with the urgent and immediate demands that you face on a daily basis that you put off your market plans. Think of marketing as the platform that you, as a speaker, stand on.

Mark suggests you start to manage your time by "imagining you have nothing to do. If your slate was empty for tomorrow, how would you spend your time? What would be the best activity in order to meet your goals in one month's time? Would it be prospecting or working on a new product? What are your top priority activities that you can complete or get a good start on in a day? It's not realistic to think you can hire that new assistant but you CAN circulate a notice to colleagues and friends. You can't develop a new product but you can create the first phase of a marketing plan."

Put first things first. When reviewing your to-do list, be sure that at least 25% of your time is spent on high priority income-generating activities and that they always come first. Put your phone on hold, if you need to, so that you can focus on just that one thing.

"Carve out a couple of hours to plan your week and then fill in all the other stuff," says Mark. "What often happens is that people go into reactive mode and spend all their time responding to phone calls or requests – in the meantime, they're neglecting their highly generative activities."

He uses a spam filter to help him manage his e-mail and finds that it frees up a lot of time. And he only subscribes to online newsletters that provide good value and content. (Of course, he subscribes to Speakers Gold e-zine!).

Observe what others are doing and take a different route. "Instead of a monthly e-zine, why not send an article to people or other things of interest to them? That's a great way to stand out. Dare to go against the grain."

Personally, Mark is fairly ruthless when it comes to managing his time. He does not own a cell phone, pager, palm pilot or laptop. Yet he works in three or four countries simultaneously with consulting projects and has as complicated a business life as anyone.

And he's a master of delegation. Mark hired six different technology people to work on creating a database and website for his company that functions pretty well by itself.

His wife says he's the only guy she knows who's on permanent retirement. He has time to pick up his daughter from day care and yet he's still earning big bucks with his consulting practice.

"I just made the decision not to be a slave to technology," says Mark. "You can be a very successful speaker without any of it."

Mark can be reached at www.getmoredone.com

CHAPTER 21

Golden Referrals
with Bill Cates, CSP

"If you must play, decide on three things at the start: the rules of the game, the stakes and the quitting time."
Chinese Proverb

Bill Cates, author of Get More Referrals Now, is a highly successful speaker who is passionate about the benefits of getting referrals.

Bill is unequivocal in his belief that the best way to build a speaking business is by building a strong referral base. The truth is, from the meeting planner's perspective, hiring an unknown speaker is a very risky proposition. Getting a recommendation from a third party reduces the risk.

"In my experience," Bill says, "meeting planners tend to make the safe decision rather than the best decision. They'll go with the known rather than the new and untried. Unless you're getting great referrals, marketing is a constant uphill battle."

When Sue Herkowitz conducted a study about how meeting planners prefer to source speakers, she found that the top three or four sources were either referrals from other meeting planners, referrals from their constituency (such as association members or company employees), or referrals from other speakers or speaker's bureaus. Referrals, referrals, referrals!

This study just proves Bill Cates's point.

"Personally," says Bill, "I've had a number of speaking engagements come from meeting planners putting out a call for speakers to company employees who recommended me. There are four main ways meeting planners prefer to find speakers and they're all based on referrals. Yet many speakers spend a lot of time doing everything other than building a referral base. They'll do expensive mailings or hours of cold calling. They'll use up incredible amounts of time on marketing strategies that won't bring them the returns that a good referral strategy consistently does."

He's had firsthand experience. He made some of the same mistakes when he first got started in the speaking business. He spent money on advertising that didn't give him great returns. While cold calling didn't get him the best results, it proved to be a little more rewarding than advertising. In the beginning, speakers certainly need to add cold calling to their marketing mix.

Another thing Bill would do differently if he were starting out today is to target a more profitable niche market than he did initially. He owned a book publishing company before he got into speaking, so his first niche was printing simply because that was the industry he knew best.

Here was the problem – printing is an industry with a low profit margin and not much of a budget for speakers, so Bill got stuck at a low fee and, more importantly, a low-fee mentality for much longer than he needed to be. Although he eventually broke out of the publishing field, it took longer than it should have for him to get the big picture and make the break.

From his wealth of experience, here are Bill's recommendations for professional speakers:

1. "Target an industry niche – don't try to be all things to all people. Find a niche that is a natural fit for you – one that has lots of potential for multiple engagements and a decent income. Some speakers have a double niche. My first niche is financial services and my second is building referrals. Put your eggs in the right basket.

2. "Be more referable. The old adage is really true. The best marketing strategy is to be really good on the platform. At an NSA conference, I emphasized that a significant percentage of your speaking engagements should lead to more business. Otherwise, something's wrong with the product! If people are not clamoring for your stuff, something needs to change. Do speeches lead to other speeches? Do people ask for your card after a speech? Do they say they'd like to have you speak for their organization? If not, ask yourself what you need to do differently.

3. "Prospect for introductions and actually ask for them. When speaking at NSA a few years ago, I asked speakers whether they called the meeting planner who hired them after the event. To my surprise, about half said no. The meeting planner spends thousands of dollars and the speaker doesn't even call back to say 'Thank you' or 'How did I do?'! They've missed an opportunity to learn from feedback, explore other possibilities and get external referrals as well. Not to mention testimonial letters which are first cousins of referrals. Prospecting for clients is all about being proactive.

4. Networking strategically. I'm not just talking about Chambers of Commerce but identifying key players and people who can help you find word-of-mouth speaking engagements. For example, having relationships with other speakers is a great networking tool. Personally, I've gotten a number of referrals from other speakers, even competitors. I consider working with bureaus a strategic networking kind of relationship. There are 100 models on how to be successful in this industry. Getting great referrals is an essential component of each model."

Part of Bill's referral base comes from his e-mail newsletter with 36,000 subscribers. In fact, it's his organization's main marketing tool and distribution piece. They use the newsletter to market their coaching program and boot camp.

They have so many subscribers that they don't have to spend much money on marketing. And although it is not the main function of the newsletter, as a spin off, they end up having a number of people call them for speaking engagements.

Bill feels that one of the best key decisions his organization made was the decision to put their training into a video training program that can be delivered without him actually being there. They now sell the training to companies.

"Banker's Life trained 3,000 people with it and paid over $100 per person which led to licensing deals," says Bill. "We have five or six of those in place with large companies, such as Merrill Lynch, who use my material in their training. This is pure profit after all the hard work I've done over the years. It doesn't cost anything to negotiate a licensing deal. I had a guy, whose license is due the end of December, who asked if I would consider selling material to them so they could use it forever. I said no. We then got into a realistic conversation, what does the next agreement look like? I like putting products together. With my background of publishing, I'm less intimidated by that process than others are."

Bill currently offers a menu of training courses, books and a newsletter. 50% of his revenue comes from speaking and 50% comes from products, licensing, etc.

Bill has created a unique and very lucrative business model that other speakers can learn from. By creating multiple streams of income, he's made himself recession-proof and by licensing videos, he's not only cut down on his workload, he's broken through the financial ceiling that was over his head when he depended solely on getting paid a certain fee per keynote or per training session.

Getting paid per hour or per keynote is the hard way to go.

You can't be everywhere at once, you just can't do it all. Creating training videos and licensing agreements is a brilliant strategy to leverage all your expertise and experience and create real wealth.

Ask yourself:

- What is your referral strategy?
- How would you benefit from adopting a more strategically advantageous referral strategy?
- Does your topic lend itself to training videos?
- Would these videos provide a benefit to your clients?
- How can you implement licensing agreements into your business plan?
- What would you license?
- What would you charge?
- How can you solidify your strategy for making referrals the foundation of your business?

Referral Strategy

_____

_____

_____

_____

_____

_____

_____

_____

_____

_____

_____

_____

_____

CHAPTER 22

Networking Magic for Professional Speakers
How to Get to the Top of Your Field Quickly
with Jill Lublin, author of Guerrilla Publicity and Networking Magic

"If I had to name the single characteristic shared by all truly successful people I've met over a lifetime, I'd say it is the ability to create and nurture a network of contacts."
Harvey MacKay, author of Swim with the Sharks

Your business depends on establishing a good rapport with your audience. Your business also depends on you having an audience. This is the gospel according to Jill Lublin. "You can be the best orator since Cicero presented his cause to the Roman senate in the first century, but if you haven't an audience, you're no more than the proverbial one hand clapping," she says.

If speakers want to be successful, they first have to be visible. And getting highly paid speaking gigs is more about who you know than what you know.

According to Jill, this is where networking comes into play. "I believe in the magic that happens with high-quality networking. When you surround yourself with the best people, you naturally attract the best engagements. Effective networking can do more for your business than any accumulation of expertise or polishing of your speaking skills. Learn to network well, and you'll wonder why you ever thought getting new business was hard."

Networking is all about building and maintaining relationships. "Effective networking involves surrounding yourself with the most caring, outstanding, intelligent, creative, and successful people," says Jill, "then actively building mutually supportive and beneficial relationships with each one of them."

When it comes to networking, it's not quantity, but quality that counts – the quality of the relationship you've nurtured and built.

"Networking means forging deep bonds as you develop a team that will support your efforts," Jill claims. "Networking becomes magical when there is an unspoken exchange of goodwill and generosity between you and your network, and between members of your network to each other. Goodwill is the foundation for making great contacts, and generosity is the soul of networking. With generosity comes warmth, kindness and a genuine delight in providing help."

Networking relationships, like all relationships, begin with you. So do a quick assessment. What do you have to offer others? What do you need or want from others? How can you create a symbiotic relationship?

"Networking is reciprocal," says Jill. "It is based on the idea that if you help me, I'll help you. You can't always be the connectee in relationships; you must also be the connector. It's a give and take relationship, where the best networkers give more than they take."

Some people are masters of the art of networking and really enjoy making connections between good people. Jill calls them matchmakers because they're "always on the lookout for opportunities to connect quality people with other quality people."

Matchmakers are highly successful in business since they have a huge network of people who are more than willing to connect them to anyone they want to meet.

How do your matchmaking skills rate? How can you take them to another level?

If you're starting from scratch, take the first step. Begin to build an effective network by finding the best people and begin introducing them to each other. "Create a comprehensive list of things people want or need," says Jill, "such as doctors, lawyers, parks, schools, and restaurants. Recognize that the best often associate with or hire the best. Carefully screen anyone you add to your list to ensure the quality of your network. Your relationships hinge on the quality of the connections that are forged. If you want excellence in your network, turn to those who do things excellently and introduce them to each other. The real magic of networking kicks in when you build relationships with the most outstanding people."

One feature the best networks share is that they are multidimensional. Rather than think of your network as strictly your target market, peers or colleagues, think broadly and inclusively. "Your network should radiate out in all directions," says Jill. "It should include top experts in areas that differ from and complement your skills. Imagine the World Wide Web, only with a personal touch. Successful networkers derive more joy from building relationships than from the ultimate increase in their businesses. They build their network on a foundation of enthusiasm and passion, which cannot be forced."

Jill suggests that you create a list of at least four or five people whom you consider the best at what they do. "Adding these people to your network will increase the diversity of your network and increase the value of your network. Regardless of whom you think you can or can't reach, set your sights high. Wonderful, marvelous, greater than expected bonuses occur when you let your friends in on your network, and especially when you let the world in. Inform your network partners and friends about your needs and allow them to help."

Jill believes that in order to build great networks, you need great people. "Include on your list the best lawyers, doctors, dentists, accountants, dry cleaners, hair stylists, massage therapists, coaches, writers, computer specialists, and any other service you've ever had occasion to use. If you don't think they're the best, expand your search to include the best people in each industry. Ask people who routinely use a service who they'd recommend. Then, ask those people whom they'd recommend for other services."

Jill recommends practicing the following three steps to develop a networker's eye for quality:

1. Develop your awareness. Begin seeing everyone you meet as a potential member of your network.

2. Clarify precisely how people you meet could help. Could they introduce you to the president of a prestigious club, or help you find the best dentist?

3. Learn to listen and observe. Asking questions and listening is the fastest path to being seen as interesting and intelligent. Besides, it's fun to listen to the best, most talented people.

Finally she suggests "Take inventory of whom you know and how they fit into your network. Make a written list of your network members, and be sure to include specific reasons why they are on your list. Effective networks are like a finely tuned professional sports team who can appear as if their coach is irrelevant. You are the coach of your network, and your goal is to get it running so smoothly you can step back and watch it purr. To get from here to there, you'll need to develop trust with people in your network."

The foundation of networking is based on mutual trust. That's one reason why it's important to be discerning as you build up your network. "You have to trust that the people in your network will always do their best," says Jill, "and you yourself have to provide outstanding service when called on by a network member or referral. Everyone delivers what is promised, honors the relationships, delivers to consistently high standards, and gives honest feedback to each other. Should any member not deliver up to your expectations, it is your responsibility to let him or her know as soon as possible. Honesty is one more gift you bring to the table as you build trust."

You need to develop a reputation as someone others can trust. "Keep your word," says Jill. "Do what you say, call when promised, speak highly of others, take responsibility for your mistakes, and always recommend the best people for each job. Remember that networking involves more giving than receiving, and if a colleague or client of yours needs assistance, you will recommend the absolute best person for the job. By referring the best people, others will associate excellence and quality directly with you, regardless of your level of participation in the job."

Another critical component of success in networking is to maintain a positive attitude, no matter what. That way, you'll automatically attract great people to your network.

According to Jill, a positive attitude has these qualities:

- Be optimistic. See everything as an opportunity or a step that could lead to a break. See everyone as a potential ally, a network partner with whom you can provide mutual help.
- Remain flexible. No matter how committed or involved you are to a specific strategy, method, or approach, be open to its failure and have some backup plans.
- Be alert. Learn to recognize warning signs and see the positive side of challenges. Look for opportunities to grow and expand.
- Be grateful and express it. Appreciate the efforts of others and make sure to tell them how thankful you are. Actively look for ways to express your appreciation.
- Shoot for the best. Always try to find the best people and then create a plan to reach them. If your top target is out of your reach, identify alternatives, but still try to reach the top.

Jill has learned from her own experience that networking can be a magical, joyful experience. She recommends you begin with a bit of soul-searching and clearly identifying your purpose – what it is that you want and need. "Clarity of purpose opens the door to possibility," she says. "People know who you are and what you want with absolute certainty.

"See nothing but possibility in everyone you meet. Every encounter you have with someone new or someone in your network is an opportunity to create magic. Then magic spills out from your generosity in these encounters, and from your gratitude for every connection you make and every person you meet.

"Aim high in your networking strategies. You always risk getting less than you want if you stop short of your ultimate dreams. Make your request known by getting out there and playing big. Take immediate and decisive action with every chance meeting or planned encounter."

And that's where the magic begins. "Once you are in action," says Jill, "playing big, giving and receiving on a regular basis, the true magic of networking will happen in the form of new friends, higher quality associates, and more opportunities than you've ever had. Think big, play big, and fall in love with giving to those in your network. No matter what happens with your speaking business, you'll always have this tight network of friends at your side."

Add a strong networking component to your marketing formula as you work your way into becoming a Six-Figure Speaker.

Jill Lublin can be reached at www.JillLublin.com

CHAPTER 23

Add Tremendous Value!
Interview with Roxanne Emmerich, CSP, Hall of Fame

"The truth is, you're not getting the big bucks for an hour long speech. You're getting paid for the transformation that takes place. It's about helping the company see life through a more productive lens and inspiring them to take action based on that more effective mindset."

Roxanne Emmerich

She had felt limited in her job. She knew she had a gift as a speaker that she wanted to make better use of. She also knew she wanted to work with companies to transform the way they did business.

"I knew I could help them massage their approach to the marketplace," she says. "I wanted to do even more than what I was currently doing and do it on a whole new platform!"

It was seventeen years ago when Roxanne first started getting paid for speaking. She met a woman who acted as an agent for speakers and the bookings started coming in almost immediately. It was a great way to start out and because Roxanne is so very good at what she does, she got a lot of referral business.

And now? "Well, after 17 years in the business, it seems I've become an overnight success!" she says. "At this point, from an overall business and net income standpoint, my company is doing really well and would certainly be in the top category."

That's an understatement in my opinion.

While Roxanne specializes in the financial field she has clients in many different industries. Her business also has a consulting arm.

Her fees are in the $30-$70,000 range for the first kick-off speech within a company. Then, most of the clients want a continued 3-year program to transform their culture, service, sales, and systems. She does everything to make sure that her recommendations to help boost the company's revenues are implemented. Since her reputation of working with business to increase their profits is golden, she no longer gets fee resistance from prospective clients.

"Here's the thing," she says, "my advice can fix the pain and that's priceless! Associations used to give me fee resistance but that happens less often now. They can see that my work creates a great shift for businesses and provides excellent value. Our company has become a household word in the banking industry. When we speak for a bank, the neighboring banks become very nervous because they know that bank will clean their competitors' clock. Just to give an example, I spoke for a bank in Tennessee whose business had remained stagnant for ten years. The next month, they had a 35% increase in business."

In the banking community, most of Roxanne's clients are the highest performing in the franchise. She balances her work with these high-achieving clients by always taking on one or two who are facing big challenges and teaches them how to look at things differently.

"These clients actually wear me out," she says, "it's all about mindset and they're often resistant to changing their attitude but I continue to do this because I always learn something from it. It's more fun working with our other clients who are highly motivated. They really get it and start high-fiving each other after the session. It's very gratifying."

Roxanne gives about seventy keynotes a year and does a tremendous amount of training on top of that. She also leads twelve seminars a year which she invites her clients to attend. She is an in-demand speaker and that's just fine with her. "I have lot of high energy so I enjoy the pace," she says.

Aside from her keynote speaking, Roxanne's company also provides a three year program for her clients. She provides them with her high end video training products and then she goes in to kick the whole process off. "I used to go on site once a year but now I'll just go out once and the other training sessions will be conducted by a high end video we've produced. Our clients are our biggest fans – we have a real love-fest with them."

At this point, Roxanne is very selective about who she decides to work with. One thing she looks for is clients who are committed. "We know what works, but they are the ones who have to implement the recommendations. If we don't sense that the commitment for breakthrough is there, we won't work with them."

Someone in Roxanne's company conducts an initial interview with a prospective client to see if they fit from a values perspective. Then she herself quizzes the executive team over the phone for 45 minutes to figure out where it hurts and ascertain if they're really willing to do what needs to be done to create a solution.

"We end up working with nine out of ten prospective clients," she says, "and for one out of ten, we suggest they attend one of our public programs. Otherwise we can't help them because they're not receptive to our advice. Our clients have to understand that we're in the driver's seat and they're on the bus. We're steering but they have to pedal and that way, we'll reach the destination together."

Clients just love Roxanne's sessions because they have huge breakthroughs. Often when she's talking to the executive team on the phone, before they've become clients, they get so enthusiastic they say 'Don't ask us questions; just sign us up'."

"As a speaker you need to make sure you add tremendous value to your audience," she says. "The truth is it's not really about an hour-long speech, that's not what you're getting the big bucks for. It's about the transformation you're helping them make. It's about the company looking at the marketplace through your lens and doing things differently."

"Start thinking about the transformation you make. I could never figure out why NSA talks about the meeting planner being a big deal. The meeting planner is not the person you need to keep happy. He or she is not the buyer. The buyer for your speech is the CEO or head of HR and the truth is, if you can help them solve a problem, they won't care about the money. Because if they don't fix the problem, they'll get sent packing. Their jobs are on the line. It's not about a great meeting—it's about a great meeting that creates a unprecedented breakthrough in a defined area. That's what is necessary."

Roxanne feels that speakers need to verse themselves in becoming phenomenally skilled in many different areas. If they're speaking on customer service, they should study different industries as well as take personal development courses.

"In this field," she says, "we always need to push ourselves. As speakers, we're hired for our wisdom so we need to make sure we're on the leading edge of change. I'm a firm believer in extensive reading. You need to simply immerse in books to acquire a deep understanding of a particular issue. Too many speakers read a book or two and think their education is over. They think they're already experts. The truth is, you need to develop a business that's more than just a gig. Audiences are highly sophisticated these days and speakers need to be ahead of them. Go deeply into full understanding."

Roxanne stopped having to market herself when she began asking "What does this client need?" and then she began figuring out how to bring it all together for them. At that point, her clients began selling her to others.

Sounds simple. It is. What does your client need? How can you respond to that need? What do you bring to the table? How much is your advice worth to your client?

Roxanne believes that if you can honestly answer that question, marketing stops being an uphill battle. "If you have a reputation for success," she says, "you don't need to do tons of mailings. You've become the ultimate purple cow that people are buzzing about because you are interesting to talk about."

Roxanne is well aware that many speakers are struggling financially. "I have a friend who's a award-winning speaker and she's practically starving," she says. "She should be booked every day of the key week of the industry she serves but she's only booked for few days of the biggest week of her industry. This year, she's already done three postcard mailings and still hasn't filled that key week that should be booked years in advance. I wish I had a day open in 2007 so I could take more of the business I want."

"She's trying to go out and wow them with her superb presentation skills. Superb presentation skills are a necessary base. However, that's not what they're buying. Speakers don't get that people want to grow their business. That's what they'll pay you for. Not for a nicely choreographed speech."

There's a great market out there that speakers need to tap into by providing great value for their clients. "Companies always have money for someone who can fix their pain," Roxanne notes.
In the beginning of her speaking career, Roxanne did some motivational speaking.

She doesn't anymore although every speech has a certain motivational component to it and clients still think what she does is motivational speaking. "Now I focus on making a difference," she says. "I'm different in the sense that I work with the executive team and help them create a plan that I expect them to start to implement right away – even before my speech. And then I say 'Here's what you do the end of the second week. So they have the whole plan – it's much more than just a gig."

You not only need to provide value for your client, you need to create a system so that your clients can measure their success. "That way," says Roxanne, "you build a great reputation and have made a substantial difference with your clients. In order to make a difference, you need to work at the executive level. We always drive that by getting executive teams to change their minds and behaviors."

As for the future of the speaking industry, Roxanne finds there's already much more demand for experts with great speaking skills than simply speakers with great platform skills.

"Buyers are very sophisticated these days and expectations are high. I see in the future that there will be more business from the bureaus and more clients going through bureaus. I think the marketing will not be so much the bureau simply sending out kits but really knowing the right person for that particular booking and setting up a conversation with the speaker. Bureaus will get close to the customers and have more of a partnership relationship with the speakers they represent."

"It used to be that bureaus would call me to ask if I spoke on leadership," says Roxanne. "They clearly didn't understand the buyer's problem at a core level. Bureaus in the future need to do a better needs analysis so that they can confidently say "Here's your person, let's talk." That way they get repeat and/or long term business. Whether you're a bureau or a speaker, one shot deals make for a tough business!"

Roxanne gets a lot of speakers asking her for help and she also hears a lot of talks about developing products just for the sake of having products. "That's the wrong approach and the wrong mindset," she says.

"As a speaker, you need to listen to your customers and when they say they wish you had something, you say "Would you like that on video? How would you want that delivered? And then they'll create a popular product line that's already pre-sold."

"Speaker after speaker writes books, creates video sets, etc. that sit in the garage. At this point, I've got lots of education tools that my clients requested. Client demand came first - I asked them exactly what they wanted and they paid for it up-front so I didn't have the cost."

"Do your research with your client. Find out their needs after an in-depth conversation and create a plan to respond to those needs, to provide a solution to their particular problem. If they say yes, start putting things in motion! "

Roxanne can be reached at www.emmerichgroup.com or
www.emmerichfinancial.com.

CHAPTER 24

Make Big Bucks Speaking
with Jack Zufelt

"I'm opposed to millionaires, but it would be dangerous to offer me the position."

Mark Twain

Jack Zufelt had three strikes against him when he started out in business.

He had no self-esteem, no formal education and no money. And yet he became highly successful as a venture capitalist, raising millions of dollars for start-up businesses. Soon others wanted to know how he achieved his remarkable success and he was often asked to share his secrets of success.

And so a speaking career was launched. Another accidental one, it seems! Jack enjoyed sharing his story with audiences so much he decided to turn his speaking into a full-time business. His aim was to hit a high six-figure income as soon as possible.

He knew that he wouldn't hit his target figure of mid to high six-figures accidentally so he thoroughly analyzed the speaking industry. Jack did his due diligence the same way he analyzed other business ventures he was considering financing. His research showed that it was not only possible to reach his financial goals but also probable, if he did the right things.

That's a big IF.

Jack started out at $2,500 per speech as a test and he got two engagements within three weeks. He quickly doubled his fee and got another engagement, so he raised his fee to $7,500 and was kept busy at that level for several months.

Jack then raised his fee to $15,000 and got booked again. His current fee is $15,000 for two hours or less. He now books events and multiple contracts for millions of dollars and recently signed a consulting contract worth $2 million.

"Anyone can do this," Jack insists. "It's all about having a marketing mindset. Speakers need to ask themselves how they can market to their target audience and to decision makers. When I researched the marketplace, I realized there were three tiers of fees: Zero to $2,500, $2,500 to $5,000 and $5,000 and over. Most speakers are in the first two tiers."

Jack's jumped right through that loop and insists that you can too. "There are six things a speaker needs to do to be financially successful in this field. First you must have a story to tell. Second, it has to be YOUR story. And third – it has to be a story that people are interested in. And that's where you start."

Like most speakers, Jack had the first three things. So what makes one speaker with a great story a big income while another, with an equally great story, struggles and does not make much money? It has to be MORE than those first three things.

The fourth element is absolutely critical. "I believe a speaker must have total confidence that his or her message is WORTH a lot of money! Now, not sometime in the distant future," he says. "I'm amazed at how many speakers start out speaking for free and then inch their way up year by year until 10 years later, they're still not making a six-figure income."

The truth is, if the message is credible from day one, speakers should begin charging from day one.

"The real question a speaker needs to ask," says Jack, "is 'How valuable is my message today?' The next question is 'How can I market myself and my message to the audience and the decision makers?'"

The fifth critical step for speakers is to put a consistent marketing plan into place. This is where many speakers falter. Unless speakers market themselves effectively, they'll end up being wall flowers at the dance. Jack notes that all the top speakers use successful attention-getting marketing tools. They also build their business on getting referrals and letters of recommendation.

"Speakers must have the ability to steadily and unabashedly market themselves in a way that causes decision makers to want to book them," says Jack. "This is not the place to hold back and be humble."

Speakers should never question their ability to present something they love and believe in for money. If they do, they question their own credibility and they are destined to experience low or no income.

"Anybody can do it!" Jack insists. "Speakers MUST acquire total confidence in themselves not just their message. Then they must learn to market properly. That's when they'll experience great financial success as a speaker. It's fun and very profitable!"

Marketing is a skill anyone can learn and successful speakers constantly market themselves. "The speaker and his or her message are the product and without proper marketing, any product will sit on the shelf," says Jack. "A big moneymaking speaker always has powerful attention-getting marketing tools that aren't just pretty but effective. I am amazed at how many speakers tell me they don't want to do any promotion or sell themselves. They say they wish they could find someone else who would be their marketing person because they just don't like doing it. Well, if you have the money to hire someone great – do it. Otherwise, do it yourself or don't speak. "

Jack's best selling book, The DNA of Success is opening doors for him and it was through intense marketing by mail and phone that he was able to get a powerful literary agent in New York who got his book published by Harper Collins.

"I had to go to New York and meet with the publisher, where I personally got a chance to market my book to the president," he says. "It was a gamble but it paid off. Marketing is crucial. You have to do it all the time."

Thanks to Jack's marketing campaign, his audio program was accepted by Nightingale-Conant and his best-selling book, The DNA of Success opened doors for both speaking engagements and training retreats.

Jack now trains speakers all over the world how to take their careers into the stratosphere and earn the big bucks that he does.

He recently signed a $2 million deal with a major company to be their marketing spokesperson. These kinds of deals come his way more and more often these days.

Jack's taken the three strikes against him – little education, no self-esteem or money and turned them into three powerful strikes FOR him. He now has a rich education although he is largely self-taught. He's got plenty of self esteem and is one of North America's most successful speakers and mentors.

The sixth principle for speakers to earn a high income is to have products.

Speakers should have audio programs and books to sell at their engagements or on the Internet as an additional source of income.

"If you don't have products to sell at your speaking engagements," he says, "you're leaving tens of thousands of dollars on the table. If you're a good presenter, your materials will sell. I consistently sell anywhere from 40% to 100% of any audience I speak to."

"Once you've created your first product, it becomes easier to produce them quickly. It doesn't take a polished salesperson to move product from the stage – it takes a great presentation. At my gigs, I sell some product to between 40 and 100% of my audience which puts an additional $5,000 to $30,000 in my pocket each time I speak."

One of Jack's most profitable sources of cash flow is through selling his products on the Internet. After meeting an internet marketing genius who taught him how to sell on the internet, Jack did $100,000 in sales in a six week period.

"I was astonished!" he says. "I now sell between $500 and $4000 a day from Internet sales. The web is a gold mine for speakers with products IF they learn how to do it properly."

Jack's success principles are well worth adopting and adapting to your speaking business.

Jack can be reached at www.dnaofsuccess.com and
www.jackzufeltspeaks.com

CHAPTER 25

The Wired Speaker
with Susan Sweeney, CSP, HoF

"Technology is like a steamroller. If you're not on the steamroller, then you are destined to become part of the road."
Bits & Pieces Magazine

Susan Sweeney and the Internet are just about synonymous. Since Susan's area of expertise is marketing online, it's not surprising that she uses the Internet almost exclusively to market herself as a speaker.

In order to get leads for speaking engagements, Susan researches conferences online and then contacts meeting planners and sends them information about her speaking topics, along with live links to her website audio and video clips.

When a potential client inquires online about her services, she checks out the company website so that she's well informed before she responds to their request.

If prospective clients have questions, she sets a specific time and invites them to attend an online meeting in her webinar facility. Susan provides them with a link to go to the special password-protected site and have an online meeting with access to PowerPoint slides that she has prepared in advance, or together they visit the client's website while Susan asks and answers questions about the speaking engagement.

What a great way to engage a prospective client and nail the booking!

When it's time for bookings, she sends a contract in a PDF format so that no one can make changes to it.

An evaluation form, an initial invoice and the introduction she wants used is e-mailed to the conference organizer well before the event.

Susan customizes all of her presentations, using the websites of audience members to make her points. Her speaking fee includes access for everyone in the audience (on a page on her website) to her PowerPoint presentation after her speech. Sometimes Susan records her session live with Camtasia software and provides a master copy of the session to the client (for a fee), or alternatively provides access to the session over the Internet for attendees.

After the event, Susan e-mails a PDF invoice and a report on the audience evaluations of her sessions along with specific comments provided by attendees to the conference organizers.

Susan's approach works well. She has a high closing ratio with prospective clients who are impressed by her professionalism.

Whether or not you take Susan's high-tech approach to the marketplace, as a speaker, you do need a stand-out website.

Here are Susan's recommendations for a highly functioning website:

- Be designed to be search-engine-friendly — make it easy for clients to access your information.
- Generate repeat traffic. Provide incentives and regular updates to get visitors to return.
- Capture your visitor's e-mail address along with permission to send them your newsletter or event notices.
- Get your web visitors to refer your site, newsletter or articles to others.
- Get visitors to check out all the pages on your site and use tracking software to keep statistics on what percentage of visitors are doing this.

Before creating your website, Susan recommends that you "Define your target markets. What are their needs, wants and expectations and discuss these with the web developer. Define the products and services you want to promote. Do a competitive analysis. Go online and check out your competition internationally. See what consumers' expectations are when they visit your website. Make it easy for the meeting planner to choose you."

The goal is to get traffic coming back to your website. Add a line to your newsletter saying: "If you want more info, check out my website," and include a live link.

Here are Susan's recommendations to convert your newsletter into a business-generating tool:

"Include viral marketing in your newsletter such as 'Feel free to send a copy to your friends.' People do what they're told to do. Without that call to action, people won't think about it. Next line should be: 'If you've received a copy from a friend, click here to get your own subscription.'

"Have an archive copy on your website so people can see what it's about. They'll see the value. Have a privacy clause. Make sure you leverage your newsletter and squeeze as much marketing out of everything you've got.

"Without appropriate mail list software, you can't do tracking or do a spam check on your material before you send it out. Take your newsletter, run it through the spam check and if the score is 5 or higher, you need to edit your message to reduce your score before sending it out.

"Mail software tells you how many clicked through to your website, etc. Add that information to the profile of people on your database. I know who asked for more info on my boot camp. So next time out, I send them a notice about the next boot camp.

"Personalize each newsletter. Schedule each newsletter so it goes out automatically when you're away. Allow subscribers to unsubscribe.

"Build your database as quickly and as big as you can. One database-building question is 'Would you like to receive my newsletter?'

"At a conference, ask everyone who wants to receive your newsletter to give you their card and they'll be in a draw for one of your products and/or services – that way you get permission to sign them up for your newsletter. You can also promote your newsletter through your signature file on every e-mail you send out.

"You need traffic for your website. You need the right model, the right website and the right traffic to be successful online. Have a strategy for generating web traffic. That might be: submitting articles to e-zines, signature files or affiliating with others. Your strategy will revolve around your particular objectives and your target market."

When people started asking for copies of Susan's presentations, she began to record her sessions. You can also do this by going into PowerPoint and instead of clicking on slide show, click a different button. The software costs $149. (And the payback can be big. One of Susan's clients bought CDs for everyone in the audience.) Download the software, plug in a microphone, click the little symbol, and the presentation is recorded. The software can also take your audio and put it on a CD.

Now you've got a product that you can put on the web where people can download it. For a fee, of course! Susan personally does a lot of private-label seminars on CD that she customizes for her clients.

"With your seminars on CD and your e-books," she says, "you've automatically got training programs. I did a series of 20 CDs on different topics on Internet marketing for tourism. The package is very valuable. I've got a search engine optimization program that consists of two CDs and an e-book which I developed for a client – I took out the customization and created the e-book now for sale on my site."

To get auto-responder software, more e-commerce information and
also to check out a state-of-the-art website,
visit www.susansweeney.com

CHAPTER 26

Mining for Gold
Making Your Website Work for You

"Make no mistake about it. Your name stands alone on the Internet and is by far your most valuable asset. This is one of the major differences between the Internet and the physical world."
Al Ries and Laura Ries

Having a well-designed and efficient website is a critical component of your online marketing strategy. Never mind the bells and whistles; the only measurement of success here is how effective your website actually is.

What returns are you looking for? And what returns are you getting? There's often a discrepancy between the two. What action do you want visitors to take? Have you made it as easy as possible for them to take that action?

Check out Chris Widener's website at www.madeforsucess.com. He gets 500,000 browsers annually. You'll see that on his home page he's linked with some of the world's top magazines. Although that's not necessarily the route you want to take, it will give you ideas on what makes an effective website.

Chris began sending articles to online magazines which resulted in meeting planners contacting him to book him to speak at events. Chris's article contained a byline with his web address. It was his website that made the sale. What can you do to encourage bookings through your website?

Many of you are also looking for income from individuals visiting your site who want your consulting services or products. You can offer a free report, get them to sign up for either your e-zine or notices of events and special discounts.

The call for action that gets the best response is simply having visitors fill out a request for more information. Visitors (and meeting planners) don't often buy or hire over the net, they want more information by phone or an in-person meeting. Put a click-through on your front page that automatically opens up to a request for more information.

Don't ask for too much info about the visitor on the form or many will leave the site at this point. They're just looking, after all. Optional fields are okay but the form should not be burdensome.

Keeping your website simple, accessible and easily navigable is important so that the browser is not distracted from taking action.

You'll get a better response to your call for action if you have your name and picture on your home page. You're in the people business and your clients need to know that you're there to answer their questions and/or complaints if necessary. They want to deal with a real live person rather than a company.

When you get the request for information, respond promptly and ask for a phone number so you can speak to your prospect personally. Your chances of getting hired for that speaking engagement go up with a personal phone call.

To increase your client base, you need lots of traffic on your website. Are your keywords current? Check out your competition's keywords by visiting their website and clicking on View and then Source. After checking out a few sites, you'll find out what keywords others are currently using and that will help you determine what is optimum for your needs.

Here are some free online tools that will help you increase your web traffic:

www.add-me.com allows you to submit your page to many popular sites free of charge, using one form.

At www.webposition.com, you can download a free trial of software called Web Position Gold that will help you build traffic by submitting your site regularly to the top search engines.

When you're submitting your website to search engines, submit the unique URL of each page of your website. For example, I'll submit www.speakersgold.com along with www.speakersgold.com/events.htm or www.speakersgold.com/products.htm

Submit your website on a fairly regular basis – certainly whenever you've made major changes, it needs to be resubmitted. The time it takes is well worth the returns.

You want your site to come up on the first page when someone types in professional or public speaker since browsers rarely go beyond the first page. This listing might be hard to get; however, you should be able to get the first page in your particular niche of professional speaking.

Another way to increase your traffic is to affiliate with sites with large amounts of traffic by exchanging links. Find non-competing but related businesses and services that you can exchange links with. Who can you affiliate with?

You can also drive traffic to your site by submitting articles you've written to e-zines. Do a search of your keywords and look for sites that publish outside articles on their site. Ask them to post your article. Or visit www.directoryofezines.com to see a list of appropriate newsletters that may want your article. Include a great (brief) tagline which directs traffic back to your website.

If you're really interested in exploring the possibilities of your website, I recommend signing up for Dr. Ralph Wilson's online newsletter at www.wilsonweb.com.

Your website needs to:

- Provide corroborative evidence about you as a speaker
- Offer meeting planners and browsers great information
- Sell your speaking services to meeting planners
- Sell your products and/or courses to individuals

More and more of your business and your client base will come from your website in the future. The speaker with the best most effective website will sweep the marketplace!

If you're planning on getting significant online sales of a product or want to promote your latest book, you'll need a separate website just for that. Your main website promotes you as a speaker and focuses on the services you offer prospective clients. It's fine to mention your book but the focus should be clearly on you as a speaker.

The second website should be dedicated to your product if it's is sold to individuals rather than meeting planners and is not tied to your speaking. Why two separate websites? Because you don't want to confuse the buyer with too many options. One site for one main option is a good rule. Two sites will also generate more traffic since you'll link one site to the other.

Another way to increase traffic and sales is to promote your website through joint ventures. You can create an affiliate program where others can sell your program for a percentage of the profits. You pay them monthly when they've made sales.

Contact some of the big names online through e-mail and ask if they'd be interested in selling your book or course. You can offer to write the endorsement on their behalf – something like "I was wowed by this information – definitely the best I've heard on how to create abundance in your life (etc.)" Endorsements by big names are very powerful selling tools.

Products not only need their own URL, they need their own sales letter which can also serve as the home page. The sales letter can be between one and eight pages with a compelling headline about the product and a strong incentive for people to buy now. It'll have lots of bullets with benefits, testimonials and a great guarantee. A 3-D graphic of the product on the website will boost sales, and so will giving browsers many opportunities throughout the sales letter to click through and purchase the product. Not everyone wants to read to the end.

My bureau website, www.speakersgold.com, doesn't generate direct sales. It's meant to generate interest. Booking a speaker is a big ticket item and sales are not made online. An intermediate step always needs to be taken.

I have a second website, www.6figurespeaker.com, that features my coaching services. Along with a newsletter sign-up form and a list of upcoming events, there are products at different price points so that visitors have an option. That website generates direct sales.

Once browsers have purchased something from you, they're now in your product funnel. Systematically follow up with anyone who's purchased anything by going back and offering another higher priced product

Offering a teaser, such as a first chapter from your book free of charge, is a great way to collect e-mail addresses.

Create an absolutely compelling headline for your book, course or teleconference call and pitch your product in every issue of your e-zine.

People buy from someone they know and trust. When I offer an e-course through my e-zine, invariably the people who purchase the course are people who know me, people who've had some interaction with me or know OF me through my former clients. The higher your profile, the easier it is to sell big-ticket items simply because people feel they know you.

By having a newsletter sign-up box and sending out a regular newsletter, a growing number of people feel that they know me. I'm building a relationship with them in a way. That's one of the reasons for putting a personal photo on your website. People then feel they know you personally and it builds trust.

Send articles you've written (with a blurb about you and your product at the end) to e-zines that require articles. Check the resources page in the back of this book for addresses of e-zines that accept articles. If you plan to do this on a large scale, there is software available that will do that automatically for you.

You can also test e-zine ads to see if they're effective in producing sales.

If you have a topic that will change people's lives or bring in more income, you'll make book sales whether or not people know you, provided you have good sales copy on your website. For larger expenditures, there often needs to be a middle step which consists of a personal touch, which might be a group teleconference call. It's not all that personal but it seems like it these days.

There's a reason why Mark Victor Hansen does teleseminars from time to time.

These free teleseminars from the man himself create an incredible increase in sales for big-ticket items. It takes an hour of his time and brings in tons of money.

Decide whether it is better to give a free teleseminar where you can then take five minutes at the end to pitch either your products or services or whether you'd prefer to have a stand-alone teleconference call that each participant pays for.

It's your call!

Consider doing a teleseminar yourself to direct traffic to your website and your products.

Use all the tools at your disposal to mine the gold waiting for you in your website.

CHAPTER 27

Advanced Marketing Tactics
for Professional Speakers
by Orvel Ray Wilson, CSP

"Successful people engage that creative part of their minds and ask "Well, I wonder how else I can look at this problem? I wonder how else I could deal with this decision? I wonder what other possibilities I have there?"

Jim Rohn

The following material is adapted, with permission, from a speech Orvel Ray Wilson gave at the 2006 NSA conference and is in his own words.

$\mathbf{A}$s professional speakers, you need to fight back with everything you've got today. This market has changed and clients are becoming more difficult and demanding. They want more and more and they want to pay less and they want it delivered it now.

The field is tough, and it's getting tougher, so we'll give you techniques and tactics you can use to fight back. I'll show you what we've done that has been successful.

In our own practice this year, we did over one million dollars of business. One of our strategies is having a seven-year marketing plan that we update regularly.

One of the trends we're seeing in the industry is a lot of uncertainty on the rise. Budgets are tighter and meeting planners are forced to do more and more and more with less and less.

Everyone wants to negotiate our fees and booking cycles are shorter. Five years ago we were taking bookings anywhere from one year to six years out. Now the average booking cycle is 97 days. We have nothing for the calendar for November and we're not worried, we know it will fill in. The cycle is shortening so you have to compete in time.

Many professional speakers have not been trained in sales and marketing. You need a strong sales campaign and a diversified marketing mix.

The days when Henry Ford said, "You can have any color you want as long as it's black" are long gone." Patricia Fripp will tell you this: that radio doesn't work, telemarketing doesn't work, direct mail doesn't work, cold calling doesn't work – what works is a combination of all these approaches. At the Guerrilla Group, we advise our clients that a marketing mix is what works.

Guerrilla selling tactics will show you how to fight back when you're understaffed and underfunded. Guerrillas thrive by using the three resources their competition tends to squander: Time, Energy and Imagination. When you don't have piles of money to spend on marketing, you need to fully utilize time, energy and imagination.

Time

It's the currency of your career, no person can outspend you. Sales people on average spend only eight hours a week actually talking to their customer. This probably also applies to you.

As a speaker, you need to maximize the contact time you spend talking to prospective clients, customers, bureaus, meeting planners. Make that first call to someone who loves you, for example, the meeting planner who you spoke for a month ago, who gave you the standing ovation and say, "I just wanted to follow up to see if your people are still talking about that." That will get your day going on the right note.

Call early or call late. If you have trouble getting through, try calling at 7 in the morning or 7 at night. If someone answers the phone, who's it likely to be?

The Golden Selling Hour, according to the American Marketing Institution is between 9 and 10 a.m. You'll have a five times better chance of reaching your party than any other time of the day. So don't spend that time doing anything else but being on the phone. You'll get more done on the phone in that hour than in four hours any other time of the day.

Automate your contact management system so you're tracking each call and know when to follow up.

You get to a certain level in your career where you have more opportunity than you can even deal with. Don't get buried in material, stand by the wastebasket when you open your mail.

Energy

Vince Lombardi said, "Fatigue makes cowards of us all." And

energy, like time, is a finite resource so eat right and avoid anything that is fatty or high in sugar. Eggs are brain food.

Skip lunch. Exercise. While on the road take advantage of exercise facilities. Authorities say that 20 minutes a day elevating your heart rate to 85% by walking, running, swimming or jogging is necessary.

Take time out from time to time.

Take a vacation four or five times a year.

Imagination

This is our most powerful resource. This is really what we get paid for. Read David Schwartz's book Thinking Big published in 1963. Read it once a year just to clear the cobwebs out of your head.

One of the big ideas in this book is that a big deal doesn't take any more time to put together than a little deal and, as Zig Ziglar will tell you, there's room at the top. Many times, because people are intimidated by big names and big numbers, they don't go after the great opportunities so you'll find less competition at that level.

It's easy to get to the top 10 or 5% of this industry because there are fewer people to compete with. Set big goals and big dreams. Five years ago, if someone had told me that I would be doing what I'm doing now, I would have asked what drugs they were on.

Use your imagination creatively.

Speakers are also writers. Make this your motto: Never a day without a line. Write something new every single day, even if it's only a paragraph. Have a place set aside for doing your writing, a place that you use exclusively to write. It becomes a discipline.

All the products you see here today first started as a wild idea and then turned into a very skimpy file on the computer. We created our first product by buying a printer for $600 and began cutting the cover apart with scissors. Then we bought labels and stuck it all together.

We made 10 of them and took them out to friends and neighbors and got feedback. People picked them up at seminars and said "Oh, how much is that?" and we said "Uh - $59." And they said "Okay, we'll buy it." So next time we said "$69" and so on.

We worked hard to find the price sensitivity by literally manufacturing the stuff one at a time until we were satisfied with how it looked. Then we took the prototype to a professional designer and said "Here, execute this." That tactic will save you tons of money.

That way, the development of your product ideas becomes boot-strap self-funding. If you put together a video you shot with your 8-millimeter and you sell 25 of them, you can now pay for a studio to reshoot it.

Create your own prototypes and find someone to execute them.

Think twice before shooting that video. It will be in circulation for a long time so you want to make sure it's professionally done. And when you send out videos or DVDs, never ask your prospect to return your material.

When we were in the recording studio, we added this comment to our video: "Please pass this information on to anyone who could use it." You'll never outlive your old tapes so keep them in the hands of someone who might use them.

It irritates me when speakers call me and say, "You know that videotape I sent you? Could I have it back please?" It's a dumb question because we're always looking for good people. Just because we didn't get back to that person doesn't mean we wouldn't have in the future.

We've had people call us four years later and say "You know, I wanted you in 1993 and in 1994 and this year, I'm going to get my way!" Great, because I've been practicing! And by the way, my fees have gone up.

Put together an idea of the week book.

The head of NCR attributed his success to this notebook he carried everywhere. It was a cheap little blue notebook and he labeled it 'Ideas of the Week'. He wrote them all down.

At the end of a year, he had 50 or 60 good ideas. Some of them were brilliant. At the end of 10 years, that cheap notebook of his was worth over $100 million in profits to his organization.

Ira never studied marketing in college and was not particularly gifted. He was just an ordinary person. His genius was that he didn't let his creativity and imagination just slip away and get lost. He captured it in writing.

You need every single edge you can find just to cut through the noise in the marketplace. Today's meeting planners are bombarded by about 3,000 marketing messages a week. Just at the Guerilla Group, I get one or two videotapes a week from speakers who want to come work for us because of the reputation we've created. I don't have time to even look at them.

In order to stand out in a very crowded marketplace, you need to use Secret Weapons.

Two of those weapons are Information and Surprise

Information and Surprise

Know more about your client, market and topic than anyone on the planet.

Surprise is showing up when you're not expected, doing what others don't do. Look at every other speaker around you, watch what they do and do something different.

Even though we all start out doing other people's material, you need to be unique. Listen to the top speakers but don't take their materials. What happens to your credibility when they hear you taking someone else's story?

Do whatever you need to do to be unique and stand out. Surprise and delight your audiences.   Always be on the leading edge, always tell them something new that they didn't know.

In terms of information, here are some weapons you can use:

The first weapon is to make good use of directories and databases. Build your personal database by getting web visitors to sign up for your newsletter. And you want every single participant in every single seminar you do on your mailing list.

When Guerilla Selling was being printed and we were getting ready to roll it out to the market, we decided to test it as a public seminar. So we went looking for people who might sponsor it, people who put seminars on. We wanted a low-risk context so we started out working with Chambers of Commerce.

There's a company in Colorado that publishes a directory of 2,700 Chambers of Commerce across the United States. It's available on disc for $285 which was a lot of money for us in 1991.

We made the investment, loaded the database on the computer and did a search for chambers in cities over 20,000 in population. That kicked out a sublist of 400 and we called up all the Presidents.

Here was what we said:

"Hi – Do you ever have speakers come in and talk to your members? Who would I talk to about that?"

"Well, that would be our program chairman."

"Let me ask you this – my name is Orvel Ray Wilson, I'm with the Guerilla Group. We have a half-day seminar on Guerilla Selling based on unconventional tactics on increasing sales. Do you think your program chair would be interested in that?"

"Well, yeah, but talk to Katie Coates – she's our program chair."

Ring…ring.

"Hi, Katie, I'm Orvel Ray Wilson and I was just talking to Darren King, the Chamber President who said I should speak to you about a seminar we have called Guerilla Selling that he felt would be of value to your membership. What's your next available date?"

She's relieved that we called and we put together a program where the Chamber gives us a small deposit and we split the take from the registration fee. This is a fee structure that we call gain-sharing, so Katie has a low-risk proposal that she can take to her board of directors. Then we work with them like crazy by saying, "Here's the brochure, here's the flyer, here's how you do the list, here's the follow-up postcard, here's the script for telemarketing" and literally show them how to fill the room.

They put 150-200 people in the room and we walked away with

our full day fee. They walk away with double that amount in their coffers. If you create a system like this, your clients will love you and tell everybody that they know.

We did 40 of these programs in the span of eight months. Every single one of them was fabulously successful and the chambers all made money. Then we took that concept to the next step and the next step.

It all started with this directory. Get a directory such as the Gale Encyclopedia of Associations or the Market Book of Bookstore. There are hundreds of them out there, check your local library.

When you're talking to a corporate client, ask them for their annual report, brochure or catalog. Many times I sit down to put together a sales training program for a corporation and I know more about what kind of a year they had than the sales manager because I've actually read the annual report.

Everything's in there that you need to know. You can find out what kind of business they're in, where all their divisions are, how many employees they have, as well as what other products and ancillary industries they are networked into.

Get the names of all the executives with their phone numbers. Go one step further and buy a single stock in their company. That way, you get to go to shareholders meetings and get quarterly updates on their company. Even better, do it electronically.

We worked with a small advertising company in California that was competing for the business of a Fortune 100 company. This Fortune 100 Company was headquartered in Chicago and there were 20 other advertising agencies in the running.

Some whiz kid in the office hopped on the Internet to see if they had a home page. They found it and started poking around, looking at all the subdirectories. They discovered that someone internally had posted the company's five-ear marketing plan. So he downloaded it, went back to the sales people and said "Look what I found!"

They restructured their presentation to match that marketing plan point by point by point so that the advertising agency could show the executives in this company how they could help them meet the goals and objectives to which they were already committed. Guess who got the contract?

Now they have a new problem – they have to hire 20 new people just to manage this one new account. You can do the same thing for your clients. Online marketing is a tremendous boon. Use it to get information about your prospective clients.

Another way you can do this is through search engines like Veronica and Archie. Some of the new ones are even faster and better.

I was doing the opening general session keynote for the Remodeler's Association National Trade Show in Atlanta with an audience of 2,800 people. I can't sleep before a big speaking engagement so I was up at 3 a.m. surfing around on the net, typing in keywords such as remodeling and remodeler's association.

I stumbled across an article by the Chicago Tribune online, not yet out in the newspaper, with the text of the speech by the President that he was scheduled to give the same morning.

So the next day, there I was, quoting the President of the Association that I was addressing from the speech that he had not yet given since it was about to appear in the Chicago Tribune later that same day.

If you want to blow your clients away, give them tomorrow's news today.

Position yourself as an authority. One of the most authoritative things you can say is, "I was just in Rubbermaid, touring their factory and they showed me the injection molding equipment they use there. Tell me about the injection molding equipment you manufacture. We have some knowledge of that field."

And get to the front lines. Before you go in to do a program, go to the factory. We insist on it. If I'm going to presume to tell you how to run your business better, then I'd better understand how your business runs.

We customize our programs extensively. Typically it takes us two or three days worth of research and this is not optional. It is built into our fees and that's why we are quite a bit more expensive than others in the niche that we serve.

As part of our contract with our client, we tell them that we expect them to give us access to their home office, their regional vice presidents and their sales staff because we want to send them a questionnaire in advance. And I'll insist on coming in the day before I go on, even if that means their CEO has to rearrange his or her agenda.

That's part of the contract. So we ask, "Will you do that?" and they say, "Well, of course we'll do that." When's the last time a professional speaker offered to do that for them? Probably never.

Get in the front line to see things firsthand so you can talk about it.

When you're pitching your services to an organization, get on a first-name basis with everyone from the receptionist on up and follow up with each person. Maintain that matrix of relationships.

And be prepared for things to go wrong!

When I was in the Bahamas for a speaking engagement, my luggage got stuck in Miami so I was stuck in a golf shirt and Bermuda shorts.

A meeting planner said, "You've thought of everything, haven't you?" I said, "What do you mean?" She said, "I was afraid you were going to show up in a suit. Because after lunch, we are going to play golf. This is perfect."

When we at The Guerrilla Group looked at the sales techniques used by top producers around the world, what surprised us was that it wasn't a matter of technique. Many times we saw people using very different techniques to produce astronomical results in the same industry, sometimes in the same territory. Instead we looked for consistencies. What do top sales people have in common that makes them super successful?

We identified some of the characteristics that made top-producing sales people overwhelmingly successful. Here they are:

Characteristics of a Guerrilla Top Producer

Consistence

Poor selling done consistently will do better than good selling done inconsistently.

The difference between an amateur and a professional is that amateurs sometimes have bad days. A professional never has a bad day. Even when they're not at their best, they're great.

Remember the difference between image and identity. A lot of us think we need a fancy videotape or to be in the Nightingale-Conant catalog. But we don't.   Our company got more business off the amateur audiocassette we made very inexpensively in 1991 than we did from being in a catalog.

We took it into a recording studio where they took out every stutter and took the applause and doubled it and put a label on it. It cost us 85 cents a piece to manufacture. We then had a 35-minute audiocassette people can listen to on the way home.

Communicate consistence with your brand identity.   Everything we send out is authentic and represents what we do. What you see is what you'll get.

Our branding umbrella is the Guerilla Group and our niche is using "Unconventional weapons and tactics." You can be niched horizontally or vertically by industry.

We are consistent with color and our graphics.   We put our camouflage on everything: business cards, workbooks, pens. To reinforce the theme, we use jungle sounds in the background on our audio materials.

Establish your identity. That means who you really are, rather than simply your image. What's your identity? How do you stand out?

Guerrilla Selling is a federally registered trademark. You need to do that early on because if you're successful, you'll have imitators and you want to protect your branding.

Build a reputation systematically. What do you want to be known for? I'm the speaker with army guys.

Put your logo on everything you have. Use toll-free numbers. We have three at the Guerrilla Group. Our business cards, stationery and order forms all have our logo on them.

Confidence

If you ask a guerilla what they sell, they'll say "I sell the best!" I am the best speaker with Guerrilla Selling in the world. You have to position yourself as being unique. Your pitch should start with "I'm the only speaker who..." and you fill in the blank.

We interviewed thousands of people to ask them why they bought a certain product and price came into play as fifth on the list. Second on the list was selection, third was service, fourth was quality. 83% said confidence was number one.

When someone hires you, it's an act of faith. For example, my car is VERY complicated to fix but my mechanic simply hooked it up to this array of equipment, looked at a blip on the screen and says "There's your problem." Well, I'm clueless about this stuff. So I asked him if he could give me an estimate and he said, "We can have you out of here in an hour or two." Right. $800 later... I have no idea what I had just bought. The same is true when your client signs the contract and sends you the deposit check. They haven't the slightest idea what they just bought.

It's an act of blind faith, so anything you can give the meeting planner to communicate your confidence as to who you are and the job you can do is going to translate into a marketing advantage.

First of all expect the sale. Just expect them to say yes. From the minute my marketing people hand the contact over to me, I start talking as though I have the speaking engagement. I say, "What's your calendar look like? I'm going to get my calendar out because I'm going to want to visit the plant. If I can combine that with a trip I'm already making, it won't cost you anything, maybe an extra hotel night – would that be okay?"

And then I ask them to put together a care package of all their brochures videos, marketing materials, etc. "Can you do that?"

And my contact sometimes says, "Don't rush me. We haven't even made a commitment yet." And I'll respond, "No, you don't understand. This is part of my process to see whether I'll work with you or not."

Always act with confidence, as though you've got the gig.

There's nothing like a great testimonial letter to build your confidence. Collect testimonial letters by asking every single client to give you one. When someone tells you that you were great, ask them to put it on their letterhead and send it to your office. Mention that you'll send them a nice gift.

Then call and thank them. Ask if you can make copies of the letter. Pick just one sentence with a highlighter so it stands out. Pick a dozen of these letters, sequence them so prospective clients just read the highlighted part. They will only read that part and they'll think you're a god. That will motivate them to look at the rest of your stuff.

Rotate the letters regularly and then create a wall of fame for yourself. Frame the best letter and hang it in your office.

Impressions

Creating a great first impression will build your client's confidence in you. While first impressions are lasting, your client's confidence will build through consequent impressions. Build a great impression with everything that represents you, with your business card, your voice, how you answer the phone.

Have you ever called your own office? What impression do you get from your message? Only one in three impressions registers with your clients and it's important to remember that it usually takes many calls to get the booking.

This field takes patience. Only 4% of the sales will be made on the first call. More than 80% of the engagements that we close are after the eighth contact we've had with that prospect. It takes nine impressions to take your clients from total apathy to purchase readiness.

Make sure you and your staff makes a highly professional impression with each interaction with your clients and colleagues.

How does your staff's phone demeanor rate? We run a blind ad when we're looking for employees. In the ad, we say "Because of the overwhelming response to our ad – we've had to automate the screening process." So we leave a message that says "Please call this number and at the tone, leave your name, phone number and a summary of your background." Before we hire them, I want to hear how they sound on the phone because that's what my clients will be listening to.

Become an authority in your field. The best way to do that is to author something. It's a great way to increase your credibility and also to create an impression on a much larger scale. You can't buy the kind of visibility you'll get by being in the Nightingale-Conant catalogs or in trade magazines. You want to be everywhere.

Last night I got a call to be interviewed by Personal Selling Power magazine and they interviewed me on two different topics for two upcoming issues. They're writing articles for me. All these impressions accumulate. It takes 11,000 impressions to erase a single negative impression.

I was standing in line at the airport and the guy in front of me wanted a first class upgrade but it was full and he was having a fit. He was taking the agent apart. I'm thinking, this guy is a real jerk. And as he turned, I recognized that he was a member of my own chapter in Colorado. You never know who's sitting behind you, who you're going to run into at a restaurant.

When you become a professional speaker, you become a professional speaker all the time. You're always onstage, the camera is always rolling so be careful. That's why UPS washes every truck in their fleet every day of the week, whether they need it or not, because of the impression that truck makes.

The way you dress is important. You don't know who you'll bump into. Dress well enough on the plane so that if you lose your luggage, you're still good to go on.

So how do you make a really great impression? First of all, write a really great talk. It takes a lot of time, crafting, editing and reediting. And just when you're sick to death of giving it, it's just about good enough to start charging money for it.

Also - you ought to be in pictures! You need to put your picture on your card, your website, your stationery.   The part of your brain that remembers faces is 100 times bigger than the part of your brain that remembers names. That's why we all need name badges at conferences.

The more familiar your face becomes to your prospects, the more confident and relaxed they are doing business with you. So put your picture in everything you do. Put your photo on products and books. If you don't have money, go to the print shop and have an 8½ by 5½ printed with your picture, black and white, up in the corner along with From the Desk of...and your name. That's all you need with address and phone number and use that for thank you notes. So your clients see your face again and again. We literally throw our business cards in the air at the seminars we do and people pick them up. People find it hard to throw out photos.

Often when I show up to meet with the meeting planner at a conference where I'm booked, the meeting planner has my picture stuck up on the bulletin board over the desk. How frustrated do you think my competitors are when they walk in and see my picture on the bulletin board? Get your picture out there as much as you can.

Persistence

All the top-producing sales and marketing gurus shared the quality of persistence. They went back and talked to prospects even if they said no the first time. Do the same. Go back again and again and again to your prospects. Keep your name front and center in their minds.

Satisfied customers are one of the most important assets you have as a marketing tool. Ask them for referrals. For some speakers, referrals are the foundation of their business. Build a referral strategy into your marketing plan.

This is the gospel according to professional speaking: follow up, follow up, follow up, follow up!

Whether you're looking for testimonials, referrals or a booking, it's critically important not to let your leads fade into the sunset. Build a solid follow-up strategy into your market plan.

Whether it's the introductory phone call or the follow up call, a written telemarketing script will out-produce an adlib script for your telemarketers by seven to one. Sit down and tape yourself talking to a prospect, edit that and give it to a transcriber and that is the script to give to your marketing people.

Enthusiasm
You have got to be passionate about what you do. All the time.

Competitiveness
Watch what other speakers are doing and do something different. When setting your fees, check out your competitor's fees to make sure yours are congruent with your expertise and your value to your client. (If you're not losing 15% of your prospective engagements per year because your price was too high, then your price isn't high enough.)

To stay competitive, you have to stay in the game. Get involved in your community whether that's CAPS or the Heart Association. Get involved with other clubs and associations where you can speak free and sell your product. Do sales training for your internal staff, your external staff and for yourself.

Write books, write articles and get them published. Set up a column in a publication. Editors are always looking for 10-inch columns a week that they can insert with good material. Offer courses at a local university or community college.

Send out a calendar of all your speaking engagements so that your local newspaper can include you in their calendar of events.

Give seminars and workshops, display your merchandise openly. If you expect people to buy it, put it out there. Do demonstrations, offer free consultations, prepare a sales presentation or hire sales people to do it and train them.

Offer a risk-reversal guarantee to your clients. We guarantee a 10% increase in sales after a year or we'll refund our fee. Guarantees are powerful incentives.

Make publicity reprints of anything you had published. Print and duplicate it in quantity. Audiotapes and demo DVDs place you ahead of your competition when you give these to your prospective clients.

Accept credit cards. We accept them all.

Consider offering a sponsorship for an event in your community. We sponsor a soccer team in our home town. It probably doesn't get us any mileage at all but we do it anyway.

Put a bunch of one-page articles together and you've got a brochure.

We have some postcards that were printed for us by Jim Rhode and his company Smart Practice. We paid $800 for 11,000 and we've used our picture postcard in all sorts of different ways – announcing events and new books and so on.

We also do direct mail and newsletters as well as gifts for our clients or audience members. We made a deal with a company to buy these little army guys in quantity and we give them away at our gigs.

People love them.

Make sure you have satisfied clients. That's so important it's worth repeating. Have satisfied clients! Then move them up the buying curve. Offer your content in alternate formats. Keynote: 90-minutes, three-hour, half-day, full-day, multi-day, or offer it in alternate media such as audiocassettes or CD, digital audiotape, video or a set of DVDs.

Offer ancillary materials. We just did a program in Wisconsin where the client spent more on my t-shirts than he did on my fees. We've made a deal to put their colors on our t-shirt. Clients love that.

Practice fusion marketing. Get together with people who have the same constituency of customers as you do. Team up with other speakers.

We went to all of our competitors, such as Jim Cathcart and asked him to tell us all his war stories. He was honored. We got 14 of the top names in sales training who contributed their material free. Now we have a premium product that we can offer free.

These are some of the tactics that have worked very well for us. Many of them will work very well for you too. Aim to be among the top in your field. There's room at the top – go for it!

CHAPTER 28

On the Road
with Kit Grant, CSP, Hall of Fame

"Everyone would like to be the best, but most organizations lack the discipline to figure out with egoless clarity what they CAN be the best at and the will to do whatever it takes to turn that potential into reality. They lack the discipline to rinse their cottage cheese."

Jim Collins

Kit Grant is one of Canada's most popular speakers. Kit's background in sales came in handy as he built his speaking business. "Experience in direct sales is very useful in the speaking field," Kit says. He feels that speakers need to be unique, to stand out in the marketplace. "Stop copying others. Be yourself! Study others and then do it differently. If you use stories on the platform, use your own real life experience. And don't be surprised when others steal your stories. You need to keep changing them in order to stay current."

The first step toward success is to make sure your platform skills are excellent and then speakers need to "identify a specific market and just focus on that. For some of you, that might be the spousal market, a concurrent session that goes on during the main gig."

As Kit became better known in the speaking arena, he stopped selling his topics awhile ago and began selling himself. Smart move. After all, his topics can be replicated but he can't be. His demo DVD is one of his main marketing tools since he got great feedback on it– 80% of his clients really liked it.

"There's a myth that if you're really good," Kit says, "business will fall from the sky.

It's not true – you still have to work at marketing, particularly at first. Another myth is that if you're new, you can't charge anything. That's not true either.

Kit has strong opinions on the topic of raising your fees. He feels your fees should be based on the value you provide to your client, not on what others in your field are charging. "Your competition doesn't stop you from raising your fees. Only you do," he says. "I waited too long to raise my fee. I find now I'm more myself on the platform than ever before. That allows me to raise my fees. My speeches are now memorable."

Kit feels that the speaking industry is changing so quickly that many speakers are not on top of it. "The industry is changing," he says, "and so are meeting planners. The typical speaker's business model that worked well 10 years ago doesn't work any more, even though CAPS and NSA are still promoting it."

What Kit finds is that convention planners typically blow their budget on a top speaker and then fill in other spaces with thousand-dollar speakers which means that the five-thousand-dollar speaker gets squeezed out altogether.

Kit advises speakers to create their own event with an association. "Create a non-dues event," he recommends. "Tell them you don't want to speak at their convention but want to hold a non-dues event that will help the association raise funds through an entry fee and won't compete with the annual convention. Then split the take with the association. Take for example the engineer's association. Call and ask if they'd like to increase their non-dues revenue. Tell them you'll give them all your marketing materials so that they can promote a half-day or full-day event. They pay your fee and any expenses involved. Give them a packaged proven process to follow to ensure success in getting their people out to the event."

Kit suggests offering the association the option of a voice broadcast or teleconference for those who can't attend in person. They'll also get 25% of your product sales. "If over 1,000 people attend," he says, "waive your fee and reduce the percentage you give back on product sales."

Kit believes that one of the reasons speakers struggle in the marketplace today is that there's no barrier to entry. Anyone can enter the field and call themselves a speaker. Clients who've been bitten are asking for more evidence these days. "They want DVDs," says Kit, "and they're also checking references."

It's no longer enough to simply say you're good, no matter how convincing your pitch. In today's market, you need to provide collaborative evidence to prove that you're good.

One thing Kit would change if he were starting out today is to produce more product sooner and capture audience information at his gigs. "I have a free newsletter which is what I call the silver level. I also have a paid subscription, which is the gold level and I often offer it free for two months. My gold program is $30 per month and it is a hit with members because it provides them with great information. There's a 10-

12% monthly dropout rate. It creates a good income stream.

As for working with bureaus, two years ago, 85% of Kit's business came from bureaus and that number has now dropped to about 65%. He thinks the drop has occurred because he's no longer the "new kid on the block."

"After bureaus place you with a client," Kit says, "even if the client wants you back next year on a different topic, bureaus will push their latest speaker. And, in general, bureaus are notoriously bad on follow-up."

Kit is busy enough that he is doing just fine on his own. He's learned from the beginning that his success depends only on himself.

To contact Kit, go to www.kitgrant.com

CHAPTER 29

Fast Forward
Meeting Planners Talk Candidly About
Their Changing Industry

"The wind and the waves are always on the side of the ablest navigators."

Edward Gibbon

Planning a meeting at a leisurely pace is a luxury long gone. Today, meetings and conventions are being put together at warp speed and anyone who can't keep up is left on the tarmac. This rapid pace dramatically affects the lead times for professional speakers.

Time frames just keep shrinking.

"It's unbelievable," says Kim George, President of LimeLight Communications Group Inc. in Halifax, Nova Scotia. "The average turn around these days is two to four months."

"Instant results are expected," echoes Jean Silzer, President of Details Convention & Event Management in Calgary, Alberta. "Shorter lead time is a challenge in terms of time management."

Calgary is growing so quickly that corporations are converting meeting space into office space, and consequently there's more demand on hotel space. Finding meeting space on short notice can be tricky.

Shorter lead times also means more speakers are hired regionally.

"Basically the lack of time," says Tom Stulberg of the Fireworks Marketing Group in Vancouver, "is because downsizing for the past 20 years has decimated the mid-management level of major corporations. Senior people don't have support they need and they're constantly putting out fires rather than planning ahead. Their response is to call a caterer."

"They never have enough time to do the job properly and rarely allocate enough money," he continues. "Instead, they just take 10% off from last year's budget. The people who used to fight for a top quality meeting are gone. The company no longer has a history of what's been done, of what's good and what's bad. Mediocre work is becoming more acceptable."

The time crunch is, in part, thanks to electronic access which has transformed not only the way meeting planners do business but also client expectations.

"I used to get an average of 70 to 80 phone calls a day," Jean says, "and now it's all by e-mail. And everyone wants an immediate response!"

Today, meeting planners, bureaus and speakers have to turn on a dime, create a proposal in a single breath, and respond to the client's request before they've even exhaled or else they risk losing the business. Whew!!

Time is tight and sometimes so are budgets, although with budgets, a better word is accountable.

Mary Anne Signorelli of the Huron Consulting Group in Chicago says, "It's no longer 'We want the best and never mind the cost.' Clients are more budget-conscious but never to the point of losing quality."

"I negotiate price with my clients now more than ever." adds Christine Z. Adelhardt, CMP, of Creative Consulting, Toronto, Ontario. "Clients want a good return on their buck. And they want it detailed and accounted for."

That doesn't mean that clients won't stretch the budget when they see the benefit.

Kim George offers her clients a menu. When they state their budget, she says, "Great. Here's a speaker within that budget. Here is another speaker who charges more. You choose." Often the budget is stretched. It's not all about price, it's about value.

Budgets have remained fairly stable and so have conference themes. The only difference is that clients don't want only entertainment, they want to be entertained, inspired and go back to the office with practical tools they can apply immediately.

"As demographics change, health care becomes a big keynote theme at conferences." says Mary Anne. "As far as speakers go, clients look for motivation plus practical tools."

A theme of simplicity is appealing these days, according to Kim George. "In these busy times, a simplicity theme works well for clients." It's like a breath of fresh air in a hyped-up world.

"We're often asked for a theme on balanced life, balanced work," says Tom. "Sustainability is also a popular theme and often clients want their people involved in the experience."

Being able to attend a conference and then get right back to work is a strong selling point these days, according to Mary Anne. "Clients try to squeeze in the conference on the weekend. They want something meaningful within the shortest amount of time. People like smaller venues and want it more personal and more practical. They also want networking and a formal agenda."

A lot of Christine's clients are in the incentive business. "Many of our conferences are being held in Mexico and South America." she says. "The hoteliers are now really well trained so you get great service at a very reasonable price."

Another trend is that more clients look for the CMP initials after a meeting planner's name. "MPI is doing a lot of work educating our clients," says Christine, "and it's paying off. Now a lot of hotel meeting planners are getting their designations."

Sometimes, though, when an inexperienced meeting planner calls a bureau and says 'Help!', the bureau has to step into the breach. "I will suggest themes and sometimes locations to meeting planners," says Kim George of LimeLight, "and who just the right speaker might be."

People don't always realize just what's involved in planning a meeting. "Now that people can book space and airline tickets online," says Christine, "They think that's all there is to it. They'll say 'Oh, my wife does catering, we can handle this'. If you want a good meeting, you need a professional to organize it."

As for the future, the truth is the death of in-person meetings has been greatly exaggerated. People will always need face-to-face meetings and the opportunity to network in person.

"At some point, there will be a wake up call," says Tom. "We believe that experience-based event planning is a critical part of any balanced marketing mix. Some companies understand and see that and they tend to be the more successful companies, the companies whose customers understand what the brand presence of the company is. My best advice to meeting planners is to have three or four clients whose business you know well and keep doing great work on their behalf."

Orvel Ray has this advice for those in the increasingly-demanding conference planning business: "Use guerilla tactics – Time, Energy and Imagination. Don't be afraid to break with convention. My favorite example is of George Washington crossing the Delaware. He took over the garrison at Christmas where he found soldiers drunk and off guard."

Staying on top of an industry that changes constantly is not easy. You need to keep your hands on the wheel the whole time. Speakers need to make sure their topic is not 'tired' and that it's still relevant. They need to be sure that they're providing excellent value and responding to their clients' needs. And here's the client - the meeting planner, the bureau, the buyer (the one who signs the check) and the audience. Satisfying everyone's expectations is a tall order and it needs to be done over and over again.

Here's some great advice from Australian speaker, Catherine Palin-Brinkworth on how to do just that – consistently.

"Focus on being of service," Catherine says. "That's where your value lies, and where the rewards will come. Get out there and give of your knowledge, skill and experience, to be of value to more people. Take your products and offer them. That simple. And claim your value. Don't discount them or give them away - unless they are worth less than the price you ask. Ask for what they are worth, and prove it.

"Good business is about the profitable exchange of goods and services for their value to their users. I've learned that when we get out and offer them with a service focus, and a genuine conviction of their value, we're in an upward spiral towards plenty."

So keep your hands on the wheel, watch the weather, note the changes coming down the pike and adapt to them. And always make sure your value proposition is the best!

CHAPTER 30

Courting the Convention Planner

"The only way to discover the limits of the possible is to go beyond them into the impossible."

Arthur C. Clarke

One thing Kare Anderson does to impress meeting planners is to offer a double header. In other words, she offers two speeches or break-out sessions at the conference she was hired to address for her regular keynote fee.

"Meeting planners want to leverage the value of speakers," she says, "and speakers want to do less marketing. You can have a doubleheader, which is two different same-day programs for a total of two hours."

So Kare offers a breakout session or a program for trade exhibitors at the conference along with her keynote for attendees. Kare also benefits from this arrangement. By getting in front of all of the exhibitors and their parent organizations, she immediately increases her sphere of influence.

"Exhibitors represent bigger companies with deeper pockets," she says, "but they're removed from the decision makers. At a recent show, I offered exhibitors 30 tips in 30 minutes on how to make the most of the trade show and many of them have referred me to the decision maker in their company."

After giving a speech, Kare makes it a point to stay and answer questions. She does a walk-about among the exhibitors during the trade show component of the conference. "I'll walk down one aisle and make comments on how they might improve their exhibits," she says. "I'll also offer the meeting planners who have been really great to me two 20-minute free consultations with exhibitors. The meeting planners can give those consultations away to whomever they choose. This makes the meeting planner look great and helps me to build my relationship with them."

Smart move, Kare. After all, she's there anyway. She's discovered a really brilliant way to maximize her presence at this conference so that it gives her long-term results.

She often also speaks to exhibitors privately and candidly and says, "Here is something that needs to change. I can show your company how to do that." "I let them know that I could come into their business and speak to the entire sales force," she says.

Kare also tells exhibitors that if they introduce her to the decision maker, she'll give them a free e-book (which is on a card she hands out). She makes it a time-limited offer by telling them that if they introduce her within two days of the conference she'll give them a second e-book. It sounds simple but this technique alone tripled the sales response they got.

Kare is VERY busy when she attends a conference that is connected to a trade exhibition. She'll go around to all the exhibitors and record two sentences from them about what they liked best about the entire conference experience. This way she builds up a whole set of quotes from different people and different companies.

Meeting planners love it when Kare tells them what other exhibitors have said. Since they hired her for the conference, she offers them a PDF version of the exhibitor's feedback once she gets back to her office. She's had a huge response from meeting planners to this.

Kare is full of income-generating ideas that simply rely on leveraging the position and power she's achieved. She takes what she's got and spins it in every possible direction. She makes the maximum use of her time and energy to get the highest returns.

She sometimes gets her speeches sponsored. Here's how she does it. Let's say that the sponsor is a pharmaceutical company with a booth at the exhibition where they give CDs about their products to attendees. Kare will offer to contribute half the content to the CD or audiotape on tips on how to get more from a trade show. As part of her contribution, she makes a time-limited offer for her consultation services on the CD as well.

When she gives the speech, the person who introduces her will say, "This speech is partially underwritten by … company who will be giving away CDs, and Kare will be at their booth for 20 minutes after the session if you have any questions for her."

This whole strategy adds to Kare's income and influence at the conference.

But she doesn't stop there. She also goes around and asks attendees to e-mail her the title of the book that has helped them most in their business in the past year. In return for sending this to her, they'll get back an extremely insightful e-mail with a list of all the books that everyone has recommended in alphabetical order.

"We once had 4,000 respondents to this," she says. "People loved it. We then sent a letter to the publicist of the top 10 books and asked for four review copies which we displayed at the next conference. Then we gave the copies away to the outgoing board."

Some of the conference rooms had a poster listing the top 10 books and one of the presenters did a session on the top 50 books. "It was more popular than mine," says Kare.

"The second most-cited book was a textbook," says Kare. "So we invited the 82- year-old author to address the group. He started crying and the video was on. It was a special moment where the honor's pure and true. It brought out the attendees' better side, which is the best thing that can happen for meeting planners. That's always the goal!"

Another suggestion Kare makes to conference planners is something that adds to the content of the conference but not significantly to the cost and that is to create an action packed panel that will really appeal to the younger people who want fast ideas and interaction. The panel could consist of three to five panelists with one speaker facilitating.

"It captures their imagination," says Kare. "The topic could be 'My best two pieces of advice for this group.' The convener needs to be someone who thinks on their feet and is smart and limits each speaker to five minutes for the best two pieces of advice. This can then be put in writing with bios and given as a handout after the session."

Great value, not much work to pull together and not a high cost either.

Finally, at the end of the conference, Kare gives exhibitors a very brief coaching session on how to make an outstanding presentation. "The meeting planner loves it because when exhibitors are happy, there's a happy conference."

When Kare was committee chair of the National Speakers Association she launched a campaign. "Members of NSA or the meeting industry were to give one specific tip of how to make a meeting more memorable. We created an e-book which was then given to leaders in the industry, along with a list of the contributing NSA board members."

Kare has some tips on how to add more to the conference where she's speaking. She will openly tell the meeting planner, "My goal is to be a real partner with you. Please ask each of the speakers at the conference to state briefly the points they're planning to make. Once you've collected these tips, ask each speaker to make reference to other speakers so there's a sense of unity at the conference."

When Kare was booked to speak at a regional real estate sales rally in Southern California, she spoke to Lana, the meeting planner for this event. Lana mentioned over the phone that she was feeling overwhelmed and overloaded. In addition to this event, she was planning two other events and her husband had just left for a two week business trip, leaving her to take care of their two young boys.

"During our phone call," says Kare, "Lana told me that she had so many things to focus on that she kept jumping from project to project and she didn't feel like she was making any progress. I offered to set up a half-hour coaching call with her to help her get clear and stay focused on what was most important for her to handle, and to clarify what she should or could delegate, put off until after the meetings, or simply let go of and take off her task list."

By the end of the call, Lana had narrowed her list down to three main priorities, she created a plan for how she could get help on the events and tasks that needed to be handled, and she created a daily ritual the help her calm down and recharge on an hourly basis.

Kare has since found her skills as a personal coach to be very helpful in assisting meeting planners. By offering a half hour of her time to help a meeting planner in need, Lana got relief and she got an amazing testimonial letter after the event that mentioned her willingness to help out. Not only that, Lana referred her to the director of events at her organization's national headquarters.

"This is just more proof in that timeless law of business that Givers Gain!"says Kare. "Now, I often ask meeting planners how they are doing rather than focusing solely on the details of my booking. This experience was gift in the fact that I discovered that I can help meeting planners beyond being easy to work with and delivering a great speech.

"We're so blessed to be part of the meeting industry," she says. "We have the opportunity to get to know people in a more profound way and we should all be part of that."

Amen....

Kare can be reached at www.sayitbetter.com

CHAPTER 31

Get it in Writing
Fees and Contracts and Negotiating the Best Deal

"Would you like to make more money? Well, go to the nearest mirror and negotiate with your boss. The person in the mirror is the one who determines how much you will earn. You are the president of your personal company."

Brian Tracy

What to charge? That's the question I am most often asked. I find over and over again that new speakers undercharge when they start out. Or, at the other extreme, some untested speakers inflate their fees based on what they see other speakers getting, without providing the equivalent depth of experience, insight and value to the buyer.

So here are some guidelines:

If you're starting out and don't yet have experience but you do have credible materials and you've gotten good feedback from speeches, I'd suggest a starting fee of $2,500 for a keynote speech. $2,500 is a kind of getting your feet wet in the paid speaking market fee. Don't stay there long.

If you're well beyond the beginning stages but don't yet have solid testimonials or a minimum of 8 to 10 excellent clients, I'd suggest giving a few speeches at $3,500 simply to get the word out there about who you are and what you do.

Collect a few stellar testimonials, put together a video and bump yourself up to $5,000 when you feel ready, or even a little before you feel ready. It's natural to feel hesitant before moving up to a new fee level.

Rich Fettke says an increase in fees never initially feels 100% comfortable. Speakers need to go out of their comfort zone in order to charge what they're really worth.

Norm Rebin says that when he and his wife decided it was time to double his speaking fees, they held their breath, wondering whether they'd just priced themselves out of the market. They found, to their relief, that Norm got as many bookings as ever.

Smart speakers would do well to follow his example, although it does take nerves of steel. You need to eliminate the bottom level of your speaking engagements on an annual basis as you continue to go after higher end clients.

When you decide to increase your fees, send all your former and potential clients a letter, mentioning what date the new fee schedule will come into effect. If you've added value to justify the increase, say so. Some speakers let current clients know that they will hold their former fees for any bookings confirmed before that date, even if the event is held later. I leave this up to you –if you're getting lots of bookings, just raise your fee and stick to it.

As your credentials and value to the client grow, bump your fee up every six to twelve months.

Will you lose your current clients? Some of them. And that's a good thing. You can't get better higher paying clients without losing those at the low end.

That's what Jack Zufelt did. He started out at a modest fee and once he got bookings and great feedback, he doubled his fee every six months or so until he got to a fee he was happy with. The clients he gained along the way of raising his fee were his market test.

The average NSA speaker charges $3,500 for a keynote. That's a hard way to earn a living. Think about it. You're hired to give a keynote address to an audience of 250 and the gig is in your hometown so you don't need to travel. You're being paid $3,500. The day before the speech, you're totally focused on the speech and getting ready. The day of the speech, you're at the conference, listening to others and continuing to customize your speech based on the conference. The day after the speech, you're probably wiped out. You've just been paid $3,500 for basically three days work, not including preparation or travel.

Let me make myself perfectly clear. This is not sustainable. If this is where you are, create a plan NOW to change it.

Most speakers struggle financially. Here's my message to you. There's no need for that. The financial struggle is not a lack of talent, it's the result of a lack of vision and of imagination.

Let me tell you about Claude Haggerty. I got a call from Claude who's an illusionist and wanted to get into the field of speaking. Most of Claude's gigs are currently with schools. Immediately, I made what seemed like a fair assumption. Claude is struggling financially.

I was wrong.

Claude makes anywhere from $5K to $7K from his gigs. He gets sponsors for his events and he shows schools how to make money from his shows as well. They're happy to split the take with him.

Claude is clearly a brilliant performer. He's also a brilliant business man. Those who succeed will be both.

Aim higher than the average speaker. What's average about you? Nothing, right?

Offer your clients more and charge them more.

Some will disagree with me but personally I believe that seminars, even when they're all day, should be less than a keynote speech – simply because a keynote represents the highest level of speaking professionally. It's educational AND inspirational AND a performance.

Fees are based on more than your experience and talent on the platform. They're based on the value you leave behind. Certain topics such as networking, nutrition, educational themes and stress relief, for example, don't normally command huge fees. $3,500 is probably the ceiling here. And yes, I realize, there are certainly exceptions but that is the rule.

Mid-level topics start out at the $5,000 mark (providing you have experience and great materials) and top out at the $7,500 level – and that jump from $5K to $7,500 can take years to make. Mid-level topics are sales, marketing, customer service, team building, etc. They are topics that often have a training component.

The highest pulling topics are in the fields of leadership, strategizing and revenue generating. The fee range for a speaker who specializes in these area is in the $7,500 to $12,500 range.

The above is just a general guideline. There are speakers who can and do break right through the conventional financial ceilings by providing tremendous ongoing value to the firms they work with. And the best way to provide that break-through-the-ceiling value is by offering a package of consulting along with keynote speaking.

If you plan to earn a healthy income as a speaker, you need to say no to those who won't pay your fee. One of the speakers I represent does very well for himself as a coach and trainer. He agreed to speak at a government function for $2,500. They refused to pay him 50% up-front, even though he did a great deal of work with them ahead of time. They also refused to pay him the day of the event. It wasn't government policy.

He didn't insist that he has his own policies. So he did the gig a month ago and still hasn't been paid and probably not reimbursed for travel expenses yet either.

Who wants a gig like that? Why on earth would he accept those terms? What did he gain?

Government WILL pay 50% up-front and the final check on the day of the event. They may not like it but they'll do it. You have every right to insist or walk away.

In fact, you have a duty.

No one client is going to make or break your career. Don't be afraid to say no if you need to. Sometimes you lose a lot by accepting less.

There are times, though, when it's worthwhile to modify your terms.

You can negotiate your fee when the event ends up showcasing you in front of your target market. Or when the association agrees to feature you in their company newsletter, recommend you to other organizations, allows the press (or bureaus) to attend, sell a lot of products, or offers you some kind of barter you can't refuse such as free airfare and hotel stay in Bermuda.

Once you've determined your fee and decided on how to approach your hottest prospects, it's time to develop some great negotiating skills.

There will be those who accept your fees without question and those who challenge them as a matter of course.

If you're still suffering sticker shock with your fees, you can bet your client will as well. Your first step is to make sure you're 100% comfortable with your new fee rate. Any hesitation or lack of confidence in your voice will be evident to your client.

Learn to be comfortable with silence (which is a negotiating tactic) after you've stated your fee. It's here that many speakers offer to reduce their fees without even being asked. The minute you feel insecure about yourself or your fees, you give your power away.

Watch your self-talk just before negotiating with the buyer. Don't think "I really want this gig." Think "I can really provide a valuable service for this company."

In other words, come from a position of prosperity rather than scarcity.

Don't think that other speakers have more to offer for a lower price. They're not you. Know your unique selling proposition inside out. Have a clear vision of your value to your client and don't allow yourself to waver on the benefits you bring to the table and the lasting value for the organization. This puts you in a good negotiating position. You need to be totally committed to your own goals and to your fee structure.

If your buyer tells you they have a tight budget, let them know that you'd really like to work with them, you'd like to see them benefit from what you have to offer. Then ask if there is any way you can work within the budget by leaving something out such as the post-program follow-up or the handouts. Offer to reduce for your fee if they pay 100% in advance or change the terms of the agreement in other ways. Offer to pay your own travel in some cases. Or offer to speak for a reduced fee in exchange for a write-up in their company newsletter if that's of value to you.

Keep in mind that if you don't walk away from any deal, if you always accept what's being offered, then you're selling yourself short. 10 to 15% of your clients should object to your fee. Then you know your pricing is right.

Remember too that bureaus don't like working with speakers who waver on their fees when contacted directly by prospective buyers.

As you negotiate for the booking, the buyer may well talk about company policy. Remember it's your company policy to get 50% down and 50% the day of the speech. (This can make another point for negotiation). Naturally it's the buyer's job to get the best deal possible. It's your job too.

Ask them what their budget is and how firm it is so you know what you're dealing with. Or ask whether there's another budget for training that could be utilized. Often organizations have one budget for speakers and another for training and publications or materials that they can draw on.

The buyer's greatest concern – more than budgetary constraints - is that your speech reflects well on him and the company. Reassure him that what you have to offer will exceed his expectations.

Keep in mind that buyers often have unexpressed concerns, reservations or questions that need to be addressed. Before your conversation, brainstorm with yourself as to what those might be and make sure you take the time to address each one. Unanswered questions can kill the sale.

Tell him other clients have been more than satisfied with your speech. Listen to the buyer and know when to shut up. If you're too anxious to close the deal, you'll lose out. Collect as much information as possible. If the last speaker was a bust, it puts you in a good position.

Buyers sometimes ask you to throw in something extra. Don't be too quick to do this. When you do concede, whether it's by reducing services or fees or by adding value, do so in small increments not large ones. Or make a small concession and ask for something in return. Absorb the airfare in return for a plug in their company newsletter and a recommendation for your services to their other branches.

Suggest that your fees only hold for a certain amount of time and that if you're booked now, you'll hold to current prices even if you've increased them in the interim. Have persuasive arguments that show that she's getting a great deal. Your calendar is filling up as you speak!

A final word on negotiations:

Aim high to start out with and you'll end up in a better position. Remember your power and don't be afraid to take risks. Be willing to walk away if necessary. Some people are just too difficult to deal with.

Beware of the overly friendly person who is not a qualified buyer. He or she can waste a lot of your time without having decision-making authority. Court your client and show him/her you really want the gig – but not at any price.

A printed fee list will have a certain credibility in itself and make your fees much easier to stick to than a verbal quote. Without badmouthing anyone, demonstrate that what you have to offer is uniquely valuable.

Do your research on your client's company and needs and take your time in any negotiation. Use these magic words often, "Well, I'll need some time to think about that – can I get back to you tomorrow?"

Don't allow your client to even suggest that your services are not worth what you know in your heart they're worth. Stick to your guns. Leave the client feeling as though she got a bargain.

She did, you know. You are SO worth it.

CHAPTER 32

A Final Word

"Life is too short to be small."
Benjamin Disraeli

Congratulations, you've actually read this book. Many who have purchased it will use it as a prop and never get around to reading it.

So you're already one step ahead. Reading it, though, is only a start. No matter where you are in your speaking career, I want you to take that second step which is the major step. Reexamine every aspect of your career.

I assure you if you close down the office, take a day or two off and simply sit with yourself and take a good long hard look at the way you're currently doing things, you'll make more money that day than you will by keeping your nose to the grindstone by sending out more kits, making yet another phone call and so on.

If you're willing to put all the pieces of the puzzle on a table and after much careful thought, rearrange them in a pattern where you're working less and earning more, your speaking career will be 100 times more rewarding.

That kind of pre-planning and creating and implementing an action plan is what separates those who do well in this field and those who continue to struggle.

So whose side are you on? Shut it all down for a day, go somewhere quiet and begin dreaming. Then sift through those dreams, throw out the fluff, keep the substance and begin to draft an action plan for the next twelve months. Let it sit for 24 hours and then come back to it, rework it and you're all set. Of course, you'll tweak it as you go. Certainly you'll try things that seem like a carefully thought-out sure bet that in fact are not a good use of your time and money. But no risk, no gain.

Once you have a revised action plan, now all you need to do is break your action plan into steps.

- What's most important?
- What needs to be done now?
- What do you need to stop doing?
- What will have to wait until later?
- What will take it over the top?

Let me know about your successes. I'd love to include you in my next book, The Seven Figure Speaker.

Contact me at cathleen@speakersgold.com or call 416-532-9886

RESOURCES

The Six-Figure Rolodex

American Management Association
   www.amanet.org

American Seminar Leaders Association
   www.asla.com

American Society of Association Executives
   www.asaecenter.org

American Society for Training and Development
   www.astd.org

American Training and Seminar Association
   www.americantsa.com

Associations Canada
   www.greyhouse.ca

BICN Marketing & Design
   www.bicn.ca

Canadian Association of Professional Speakers
   www.canadianspeakers.org

Canadian ISBN Agency
   www.collectionscanada.ca

Canadian Non-profits
   www.charityvillage.com

Canadian Special Events
    www.canadianspecialevents.com

Career Track
    www.pryor.com

Encyclopedia of Foundations
    www.greenwood.com

Hotel Sales & Marketing Association
    www.hsmai.com

Independent Meeting Planners
    www.impaccanada.com

Institute of Management Consultants
    www.imcusa.org

Medical Meetings
    www.medicalconferences.com

Meeting Professionals International
    www.mpiweb.org

Meetings Canada Directory
    www.meetingscanada.com

National Trade & Professional Associations U.S
    www.columbiabooks.com

National Speakers Association
    www.nsaspeaker.net

Robert Reed Publishers
    www.rdrpublishers.com

Society of Incentive & Travel Executives
    www.site-intl.org

Society of Corporate Meeting Planners
    www.scmp.org

Society of Government Meeting Professionals
    www.sgmp.org

Sources Media Directory
 www.sources.com

The Yearbook of Experts and Authorities
 www.expertclick.com

Toastmasters
 www.toastmaster.org

U. S. Companies
 www.hoovers.com

U. S. Conferences
 www.allconferences.net

U. S. non-profits
 www.guidestar.org

Database Management
 www.act.com
 or
 www.filemaker.com

RECOMMENDED READING

101 Ways To Promote Your Website
By Susan Sweeney
Maximum Press
ISBN 1-931644-21-7

By Duty Bound
Survival and Redemption in Vietnam
By Brig. Gen. Ezell Ware, Jr (CA,RET)

Canadian Copyright Law
By Lesley Ellen Harris
McGraw-Hill Ryerson
McGraw-Hill
ISBN 0-07-560369-1

Confessions of Shameless Self-Promoters
By Debbie Allen
ISBN 0-9650965-5-6

Endless Referrals:
Network Your Everyday Contacts into Sales
By Bob Burg
McGraw Hill
ISBN 0-07-14627-4

From Good to Great
by Jim Collins
Harper Collins
ISBN 0-06-662099-6

Get More Referrals Now
By Bill Cates
McGraw-Hill
ISBN 0-07-141775-3

Getting Started in Speaking, Training or Seminar Consulting
By Robert Bly
Wiley
ISBN 0-471-38882-3

Guerrilla Publicity:
Hundreds of Sure-fire Tactics to Get Maximum Sales
for Minimum Dollars
By Jay Conrad Levinson, Rick Frishman and Jill Lublin
Adams Media Corporation
ISBN 1-58-62-682-3

How to Sell Anything to Anybody
by Joe Girard
Fireside Books
ISBN 978-0-7432-7396-1

How to Self-Publish and Make Money:
Writing, Publishing and Selling your Book in Canada
By Crook & Wise
Sandhill Book Marketing Ltd.
ISBN 0-920923-10-0

Instant Income
By Janet Switzer
McGraw-Hill
ISBN-13 978-0-07-148778-8

Money Talks
By Alan Weiss
McGraw-Hill
ISBN 0-07-069615-2

Never Say No Comment
By Ian Taylor and George Olds
LB Publishing
ISBN 0-9697369-3-2

Secrets of Successful Telephone Selling:
How to Generate More Leads, Sales, Repeat Business
and Referrals by Phone
By Robert W. Bly
Owl Books
ISBN 0-8050-4098-6

Seven Years to Seven Figures:
The Fast-Track Plan to Becoming a Millionaire
By Michael Masterson
Wiley & Sons
ISBN 0-471-78675-6

Speaking for Millions:
How to Make Really Big Money as a Professional Speaker
By Fred Gleeck
Fast Forward Press
ISBN 0-936965-03-7

The 4-Hour Workweek
By Timothy Ferriss
Crown Publishers
978-0-307-35313-9

The Aladdin Factor
By Jack Canfield and Mark Victor Hansen
Berkley
ISBN 0-425-15075-5

The Border Guide:
A Guide to Living, Working and Investing Across the Border
By Robert Keats
Self-Counsel Press
ISBN 1-55180-765-3

The Confident Speaker
Harrison Monarth and Larina Kase
McGraw-Hill
ISBN 13:978-0-07-148149-6

The Complete Guide to Self-Publishing
By Tom and Marilyn Ross
Writer's Digest Books
ISBN 0-89879-646-6

The Healthy PC
Carey Holzman
McGraw Hill Osborne
ISBN 0-07-222923-3

The How of Wow:
A Guide to Giving A Speech That Will Positively Blow 'Em Away
By Tony Carlson
ISBN 9 780814 472514

The Magic of Thinking Big
By David J. Schwartz, Ph.D.
Wilshire Book Company
ISBN 0-87980-092-5

The $100,000 Writer
By Nancy Flynn
Adams Media
ISBN 9-781580

The Successful Coach:
Insider Secrets to Becoming a Top Coach
By Terri Levine, Larine Kase, Joe Vitale
ISBN 0-471-78996-8

Write the Perfect Book Proposal
By Jeff Herman and Deborah Adams
Wiley
ISBN 0-471-57517-8

Yes You Can!
Behind the Hype and Hustle of the Motivation Biz
Jonathan Black
ISBN 1-59691-000-3

<u>NOTES</u>

NOTES

NOTES

ROBERT D. REED PUBLISHERS ORDER FORM

Call in your order for fast service and quantity discounts!
(541) 347- 9882

OR order on-line at www.rdrpublishers.com using PayPal.
OR order by mail: Make a copy of this form; enclose payment information:
Robert D. Reed Publishers
1380 Face Rock Drive, Bandon, OR 97411
Note: Shipping is $3.50 1st book + $1 for each additional book.

Send indicated books to:
Name: _____
Address: _____
City: _____ State: _____ Zip: _____
Phone: _____ Fax: _____ Cell: _____
E-Mail: _____
Payment by check ☐ or credit card ☐ *(All major credit cards are accepted)*
Name on card: _____
Card Number: _____
Exp. Date: _____ Last 3-Digit number on back of card: _____
Quantity: _____ Total Amount: _____

The Six-Figure Speaker:
Formula for a Six-Figure Income as a Professional Speaker
by Cathleen Fillmore ....$19.95 _____

Handling Employment BS
by Geoffrey Hopper .... $19.95 _____

100 Ways to Create Wealth
by Steve Chandler & Sam Beckford............................... $24.95 _____

The Small Business Millionaire
by Steve Chandler & Sam Beckford............................. $11.95 _____

Customer Astonishment
by Darby Checketts ....$14.95 _____

Ten Commitments for Building High Performance Teams
by Tom Massey .... $11.95 _____

Other book title(s) from website:
_____ $ _____
_____ $ _____